RISKPRO's

SANCTIONS SCREENING

A Key Element of AML and Financial Crime Prevention

© **CA Mayur Joshi**

Vedant Sangit

Certified Anti Money Laundering Expert

D1607723

© RISKPRO

ISBN 978-1-329-02502-8

Price: $50

Printed in India

Published by:

Riskpro Publication

Riskpro Management Consulting Pvt Ltd

209,Indulal Commercial Complex, L.B.Shastri Road,Navi Peth,

Pune-411030 India

Visit us at **www.riskprolearning.com**

The book is authored by CA Mayur Joshi and Vedant Sangit– Certified Anti Money Laundering Expert. For any questions relating to the books author can be reached at contactus@riskpro.co.in

TABLE OF CONTENTS

Chapter 1

BACKGROUND OF SANCTIONS

Sanctions are penalties regarding financial or commercial activities. A country or group of countries may put sanctions on another country, a group of people or organizations, or even an individual person.

WHAT ARE SANCTIONS?

In fact, multiple national governments and international bodies such as the United Nations and European Union have imposed economic sanctions to deter, punish, or shame countries or entities that endanger their interests or violate international norms of behaviour. Sanctions have been used to advance a range of foreign policy goals, including counterterrorism, counternarcotics, non-proliferation, democracy and human rights promotion, conflict resolution, and cybersecurity.

HISTORY OF SANCTIONS

Economic sanctions were not defined properly until the 20th Century. However, there are instances of similar events occurring in history. In fact, the earliest recorded instance of a sanction was in 432 BC. Sources show that the Athenian Empire of Greece placed a ban on traders and salesmen from the city of Megara from its bustling marketplace. The Megaran traders depended greatly on their access to the Athenian markets to facilitate the flow of money to and from Megara. With this action, Athens managed to deal a heavy blow to its rival's economy[i].

In the modern era, sanctions have been used as a tool of foreign policy to achieve political or diplomatic goals. The League of Nations, created after World War I, used economic sanctions against Italy in 1935 after it invaded Ethiopia. However, these sanctions failed to prevent the aggression and ultimately led to the collapse of the League.

In the post-World War II era, the United States and its allies used economic sanctions against communist countries, including the Soviet Union and Cuba, as a way of containing the spread of communism. Economic sanctions were also used during the Cold War to target rogue states like North Korea, Iraq, and Iran.

In the 1990s, the United Nations Security Council began to play a more prominent role in imposing sanctions against countries that violated international norms, such as Iraq after its invasion of Kuwait in 1990. Since then, the UN has used sanctions to address a range of issues, including human rights abuses, nuclear proliferation, and terrorism.

For most of history, sanctions involved governments choosing to physically block or embargo trade intended for another nation. Sanctions began to evolve to their current state near the end of the 19th century. Within Europe, peace societies began to discuss the evils of war and pacifist alternatives.

Sanctions saw a significant rise in the 20th Century, primarily driven by the efforts of international organizations like the United Nations and the League of Nations. These organizations employed political and financial strategies to compel non-compliant nations to adhere to their policies and to penalize those who violated their guidelines. Over time, these measures transformed into country-specific sanctions, which are imposed as a response to severe offenses and serve as a form of retaliation.

HOW DO SANCTIONS WORK?

Economic Sanctions have the most devastating effect on the country they are put on. Governing bodies usually impose economic sanctions on offending countries to prevent them from trading with other countries. They may also increase the import duties on certain goods significantly. This causes economic loss to the importer and discourages them from participating in trade. It aims to disrupt the economic stability of the country in order to force them to comply with guidelines and repent for their digressions. However, it may also affect neutral countries that depend on certain goods and services from the stigmatized country.

TYPES OF SANCTIONS

There are different types of sanctions, that may be imposed depending on the circumstances. Either an individual or a group such as a governing state or a country may find themself to be the subject of sanctions.

ECONOMIC SANCTIONS

Economic sanctions are a form of punitive measure used by governments, usually against other countries or their governments, to achieve a particular political, economic or social goal. Economic sanctions typically involve a wide range of measures, including trade restrictions, asset freezes, and financial transaction bans. These measures are intended to create economic and political pressure on the target country, to force it to change its behaviour or policies.

A very prevalent example of economic sanctions in recent times is the United States and many aligning countries refusing to export to or import any goods from Russia after its atrocities against Ukraine. The United States and EU restricted Russian companies' access to international capital markets by limiting their ability to issue debt or equity.

They also prohibited the export of certain technologies to Russia, including technologies related to the oil and gas sector, military equipment, and dual-use goods.

The United States and EU also froze the assets and imposed travel bans on a number of Russian officials and businessmen who were deemed to be involved in the Ukraine conflict.

The EU imposed restrictions on energy sector cooperation with Russia, including a ban on the import of certain oil and gas-related technologies. However, the effectiveness of the sanctions in changing Russia's behavior has been a subject of debate. While the sanctions did put pressure on the Russian government, they did not succeed in stopping Russian aggression.

The aim of economic sanctions can vary depending on the situation, but some common objectives include:

- Changing the behavior or policies of the targeted entity: Economic sanctions can be used to coerce a targeted country or government into changing its behavior or policies. For example, sanctions may be imposed to pressure a government to stop human rights abuses, end its support for terrorism, or abandon its nuclear weapons program.

- Promoting democracy and human rights: Sanctions can also be used to promote democracy and human rights. For instance, sanctions may be imposed to pressure a government to hold free and fair elections, respect the rule of law, or release political prisoners.

- Protecting national security: Economic sanctions can be used to protect national security by preventing the targeted country or government from acquiring weapons, technology, or other resources that could pose a threat to the sanctioning country or its allies.

- Sending a message: Sanctions can also be used to send a message to the targeted entity and others that certain actions or behaviors will not be tolerated by the international community.

DIPLOMATIC SANCTIONS

Diplomatic sanctions are a form of punishment or pressure that one country or group of countries can impose on another by reducing or cutting off diplomatic ties. Diplomatic sanctions can take various forms, such as

- expelling diplomats,

- recalling one's own ambassadors, and
- prohibiting high-level diplomatic visits.

Diplomatic sanctions can be used to express disapproval of a particular government's actions, policies, or behavior, and to signal to the offending government that it is isolated and lacks international support. In some cases, diplomatic sanctions can be a precursor to more severe actions, such as economic sanctions or military intervention. It's important to note that diplomatic sanctions are different from economic sanctions, which aim to restrict or prevent trade and financial transactions with a country or group of countries. While diplomatic sanctions do not have a direct impact on a country's economy, they can still have significant diplomatic consequences and can be a powerful tool for expressing disapproval or applying pressure on a particular government.

SANCTIONS ON INDIVIDUALS

Some bodies like the United Nations have the ability to put them on individuals. In this case, individuals refer to those who they view as threats to the world's peace and integrity. The most common recipients of it are dangerous political leaders, financial criminals who may affect the economy and terrorists.

SANCTIONS REGARDING THE ENVIRONMENT

Due to rising concerns about environmental issues such as global warming and deforestation, some countries may come together and enact it and trade barriers restricting the use of certain natural resources. Some countries may cause harm to endangered species and wildlife via their trading or development methods. In these cases, they may face sanctions. For instance, the UNSC sanctions against North Korea in 2017 included a ban on the export of coal, iron, lead, and seafood, which were also contributing to environmental degradation in the country, in addition to their role in funding North Korea's nuclear and ballistic missile programs.

MILITARY SANCTIONS

"Military sanctions" is not a commonly used term in international relations or diplomacy. The term "sanctions" generally refers to measures taken by one country or group of countries against another country or entity, such as economic or diplomatic sanctions.

However, it's possible that "military sanctions" could refer to the use of military force as a form of punishment or pressure against another country. In this context, military sanctions could include actions such as imposing a no-fly zone over a country, conducting airstrikes, or deploying military forces to a particular area as a show of force.

It's worth noting that the use of military force as a form of sanctions is highly controversial and can have serious consequences, both in terms of human life and international relations. Therefore, it is typically viewed as a last resort and is only used in extreme circumstances.

SPORTS SANCTIONS

Sports sanctions are restrictions imposed on a particular country's sports teams or athletes. These restrictions may include disqualifying a country's team or athletes from participating in international sporting events such as the Olympics, World Cup, or other tournaments. Sports sanctions can be imposed for various reasons, such as human rights violations, discrimination, or geopolitical tensions between nations. In some cases, sports sanctions may be used as a form of diplomatic pressure to influence the policies of a country or to express disapproval of its actions.

For example, the 2022 Wimbledon Championship has banned all Russian and Belarusian players from competing. This included the then World No.2 Daniil Medvedev, who is Russian.

TRAVEL SANCTIONS

Travel sanctions are a type of sanction that restricts or prohibits travel to a specific country or entity. They are often used as a tool of foreign policy to punish individuals or entities that are involved in illegal or illicit activities, such as human rights abuses, terrorism, or nuclear proliferation.

Travel sanctions can take several different forms, including visa bans, travel restrictions, and passport revocations. Visa bans are a common type of travel sanction, which involves denying visas to individuals who are deemed to be a security threat or involved in illegal activities. Travel restrictions can include limitations on the number of times an individual can travel to a country, the duration of their stay, or the purpose of their visit. Passport revocations involve cancelling an individual's passport, making it impossible for them to travel internationally.

Travel sanctions can have a significant impact on individuals and their families, particularly those who have legitimate reasons for travel, such as medical treatment or education. In some cases, travel sanctions can also impact business or academic travel, leading to economic or intellectual consequences.

While travel sanctions can be effective in isolating and punishing individuals involved in illegal or illicit activities, they have also been criticized for their impact on innocent individuals who may be caught up in the sanctions. Additionally, travel sanctions may not always achieve their intended goals, as individuals may find ways to circumvent the sanctions or travel to other countries instead. Therefore, travel sanctions are often used in combination with other types of sanctions and diplomatic efforts to achieve their intended goals.

WHO IMPOSES SANCTIONS?

Individual states, the United Nations Security Council, the North Atlantic Treaty Organization and the European Union are the most important bodies that can impose sanctions.

The UN sanctions mostly target countries that threaten the natural peace and harmony between the countries of the world, or which don't cooperate with their policies. Breaching any imposed sanctions counts as a criminal offence.

SANCTIONS BY INTERNATIONAL ORGANIZATIONS

International organizations can impose sanctions to pressure governments or other entities to comply with international law, treaties, or norms. These organizations may include the United Nations, the European Union, the World Trade Organization, and others.

UN SECURITY COUNCIL

The United Nations is a key international organization that can impose sanctions. The UN Security Council can impose sanctions on countries or entities that threaten international peace and security, and it can also authorize the use of force to enforce those sanctions. The UN may also impose sanctions related to human rights violations, terrorism, and the proliferation of weapons of mass destruction.

The United Nations Security Council (UNSC) employs several criteria for targeting individuals and entities with sanctions, which are outlined in its various resolutions. The main criteria include:

- Threats to international peace and security: The UNSC can impose sanctions on individuals or entities that pose a threat to international peace and security, such as those involved in terrorism, the proliferation of weapons of mass destruction, or the violation of human rights.

- Violations of international law: The UNSC can also impose sanctions on individuals or entities that have violated international law, including UN resolutions or international humanitarian law.

- Obstruction of peace processes: The UNSC can impose sanctions on individuals or entities that obstruct peace processes or negotiations, including those involved in conflict or destabilization of a region.

- Support for illegal activities: The UNSC can impose sanctions on individuals or entities that provide financial or other support for illegal activities, such as drug trafficking or organized crime.

- Non-compliance with UN resolutions: The UNSC can impose sanctions on individuals or entities that fail to comply with UN resolutions, including those related to weapons proliferation, terrorism, or human rights.

- Interference in the affairs of another country: The UNSC can impose sanctions on individuals or entities that interfere in the internal affairs of another country, including through acts of aggression or the provision of support to armed groups.

In addition to these criteria, the UNSC may also consider the potential impact of sanctions on the affected individuals, entities, and populations, as well as the effectiveness of the sanctions in achieving their intended goals. The UNSC typically relies on the reports of its sanctions committees, which monitor the implementation and effectiveness of sanctions, to inform its decision-making.

EUROPEAN UNION

The European Union can also impose economic and diplomatic sanctions on countries and entities that violate international law or threaten the security of the EU or its member states. These sanctions can include trade restrictions, asset freezes, and travel bans. The EU may also impose sanctions related to human rights violations, terrorism, and the use of chemical weapons.

The European Union (EU) can impose sanctions on individuals, entities, or countries under several criteria, which are outlined in its Common Foreign and Security Policy (CFSP) and in relevant legislation. CFSP is defined in the EU's governing treaties and is designed to promote the EU's interests and values in its external relations with other countries and international organizations.

Under the CFSP, the EU seeks to promote peace, security, and stability in its neighborhood and beyond, and to work towards common solutions to global challenges, such as terrorism, climate change, and poverty. EU imposes the sanctions when it notices human rights violations, terrorist activities, proliferation of weapons, acts of aggression or support to cyberattacks. The EU also takes into account the potential impact of sanctions on the affected individuals, entities, and populations, as well as the effectiveness of the sanctions in achieving their intended goals. The EU typically relies on its Foreign Affairs Council and the High Representative for Foreign Affairs and Security Policy to decide on sanctions and their scope, and on the European External Action Service to implement and monitor their effectiveness.

The EU has also imposed a range of sanctions on Iran over its nuclear program, including asset freezes, travel bans, and restrictions on trade and investment in key sectors, such as oil and gas. These sanctions were lifted in 2016 after the conclusion of the Joint Comprehensive Plan of Action (JCPOA), but some were re-imposed by the EU in 2018 following the US withdrawal from the JCPOA.

BUREAU OF INDUSTRY AND SECURITY

The Bureau of Industry and Security (BIS) is an agency within the United States Department of Commerce that is responsible for implementing and enforcing U.S. export control regulations. BIS is tasked with promoting U.S. national security, foreign policy, and economic objectives by ensuring that sensitive technologies and goods are not exported to countries, organizations, or individuals that pose a threat to U.S. interests. BIS is responsible for administering certain sanctions programs that are implemented under the Export Administration Regulations (EAR), which govern the export, reexport, and transfer of certain commodities, software, and technology from the U.S. to foreign countries.

Under the EAR, BIS may impose licensing requirements or other restrictions on exports to countries that are subject to U.S. sanctions, such as Iran, North Korea, and Syria. BIS is also responsible for enforcing sanctions that target specific individuals, organizations, or entities, such as those listed on the Entity List or the Denied Persons List. In addition to administering sanctions under the EAR, BIS also plays a role in coordinating with other U.S. agencies, such as the Office of Foreign Assets Control (OFAC) and the Department of State, to ensure that U.S. sanctions policies are implemented effectively and consistently. BIS works with these agencies to identify and target entities and individuals that violate U.S. sanctions, and to develop and implement strategies for addressing emerging threats to U.S. national security.

OFAC SANCTIONS

The Office of Foreign Assets Control (OFAC) is an agency within the U.S. Department of the Treasury that is responsible for administering and enforcing U.S. economic sanctions programs.

OFAC plays a key role in implementing U.S. sanctions policy by blocking assets of targeted individuals, organizations, and countries, and by prohibiting U.S. persons from engaging in certain transactions with them. U.S. sanctions policies are designed to promote U.S. interests and values by restricting certain types of transactions with targeted countries, entities, and individuals. The specific goals and measures of these policies may vary depending on the context and the priorities of U.S. policymakers.

The specific goals of U.S. sanctions policies can vary depending on the context, but generally include:

Promoting democracy, human rights, and the rule of law: U.S. sanctions policies are often used to target countries and individuals that engage in human rights abuses, corruption, or other activities that undermine democracy or the rule of law.

- Countering terrorism and other security threats: U.S. sanctions policies may be used to target individuals or organizations that are involved in terrorism, proliferation of weapons of mass destruction, or other activities that pose a threat to U.S. national security.

- Addressing regional conflicts and instability: U.S. sanctions policies may be used to address regional conflicts and instability, such as those in the Middle East, North Korea, or Ukraine.

- Protecting U.S. economic interests: U.S. sanctions policies may be used to protect U.S. economic interests by targeting entities that engage in unfair trade practices or other activities that harm U.S. businesses.

OFAC maintains and enforces a number of different sanctions programs, which target countries, entities, and individuals that pose a threat to U.S. national security, foreign policy, or economic interests. These sanctions may include asset freezes, travel bans, and prohibitions on U.S. persons engaging in transactions with sanctioned individuals or entities. OFAC also maintains a list of Specially Designated

Nationals and Blocked Persons (SDN List), which identifies individuals and entities that are subject to U.S. sanctions.

INTERPOL

Interpol, the International Criminal Police Organization, plays a role in sanctions enforcement by providing law enforcement agencies around the world with tools and resources to assist in identifying and apprehending individuals and entities subject to sanctions.

Interpol's role in sanctions enforcement includes:

- Red Notices: Interpol issues Red Notices at the request of member countries to alert law enforcement agencies around the world that an individual is wanted for prosecution or to serve a sentence. Red Notices can be used to enforce sanctions by alerting law enforcement agencies to individuals subject to sanctions.

- Border Control: Interpol provides training and support to border control authorities to help them identify individuals subject to sanctions and prevent their entry into countries where they are prohibited.

- Information Sharing: Interpol provides a platform for member countries to share information about individuals and entities subject to sanctions, allowing law enforcement agencies to more effectively identify and target these individuals.

- Asset Recovery: Interpol also provides support for asset recovery efforts related to sanctions enforcement. Interpol can assist with identifying and tracing assets that have been acquired through illicit activities, and can help facilitate cooperation between law enforcement agencies and financial institutions to freeze and seize these assets.

WORLD TRADE ORGANISATION

The World Trade Organization (WTO) can impose sanctions on countries that violate WTO rules and agreements. These sanctions can include increased tariffs on imports from the offending country or restrictions on that country's exports to other WTO members.

Other international organizations, such as the African Union, the Organization of American States, and the Association of Southeast Asian Nations, may also impose sanctions to promote regional security and stability or to advance shared values and norms.

Sanctions imposed by international organizations can be powerful tools for enforcing international law and norms, but they can also be controversial and may have unintended consequences. Critics argue that sanctions can harm innocent civilians and undermine diplomatic efforts to resolve conflicts peacefully.

The United Nations has imposed multiple rounds of sanctions on North Korea in response to its nuclear weapons and ballistic missile programs. The sanctions have targeted North Korea's weapons-related trade, luxury goods, and financial transactions. The UN also imposed travel bans and asset freezes on North Korean individuals and entities that were deemed to be involved in the country's nuclear and missile programs.

SANCTIONS BY GOVERNMENTS

Governments can impose sanctions as a way to express disapproval, to bring about political change, or to compel compliance with international norms or treaties. These sanctions can be implemented unilaterally or as part of a coordinated effort with other countries or international organizations.

Some common types of sanctions that governments can impose include:

- Trade sanctions: Governments can limit or prohibit the import or export of goods, services, and technologies from or to a targeted country. This can include restrictions on the sale of arms, military equipment, and other strategic goods.

- Financial sanctions: Governments can freeze assets, block financial transactions, and prohibit investments in a targeted country. This can have a significant impact on a country's economy and its ability to engage in international trade and commerce.

- Travel sanctions: Governments can restrict the travel of individuals from a targeted country. This can include denying visas or travel permits to government officials, business leaders, and other individuals.

- Diplomatic sanctions: Governments can expel diplomats, close diplomatic missions, or reduce diplomatic relations with a targeted country. This can limit the ability of the targeted country to engage in international diplomacy and conduct foreign policy.

- Other sanctions: Governments can also impose other types of sanctions, such as cultural, scientific, or educational sanctions. These can include restrictions on academic exchanges, cultural events, or scientific cooperation with a targeted country.

The effectiveness of government sanctions can vary depending on a variety of factors, including the strength of the economy, the political stability of the targeted country, and the degree of international support for the sanctions. In some cases, sanctions may result in the desired political change or compliance, while in other cases, they may be ineffective or even counterproductive.

In 2019, the United States imposed sanctions on Venezuela in response to what it deemed to be fraudulent elections and human rights abuses. The US targeted the Venezuelan oil sector, which was a major source of revenue for the country, as well as individuals and entities that were deemed to be supporting the government of President Nicolas Maduro.

SPORTS ORGANIZATIONS

Sports organizations may impose sanctions to penalize individuals, teams, or countries that violate their rules and regulations. Some examples of sanctions imposed by sports organizations include:

- Bans on participation: Sports organizations may ban individuals or teams from participating in their events or competitions as a result of a rule violation. For example, the International Association of Athletics Federations (IAAF) banned the Russian Athletics Federation from participating in international competitions in 2015 following allegations of state-sponsored doping.

- Fines: Sports organizations may impose fines on individuals or teams that violate their rules. For example, the International Olympic Committee (IOC) fined the Chinese badminton team in 2012 for "not using one's best efforts to win a match" during the London Olympics.

- Stripping of medals or titles: Sports organizations may strip individuals or teams of medals or titles if they are found to have violated rules or regulations. For example, Lance Armstrong was stripped of his seven Tour de France titles in 2012 for doping.

- Suspension: Sports organizations may suspend individuals or teams from participating in their events or competitions for a certain period of time. For example, FIFA suspended Uruguay's Luis Suarez from all football-related activities for four months in 2014 for biting an opponent during the World Cup.

- Points deduction: In team sports, sports organizations may deduct points from a team's score as a penalty for violating their rules. For example, the English Football Association deducted nine points from Birmingham City's total in 2019 for violating financial regulations.

Sanctions imposed by sports organizations can have a significant impact on individuals, teams, and countries, as they may result in lost opportunities, revenue, and reputation.

Practice Questions

What are economic sanctions?

A. Measures taken to restrict or prohibit travel to a country or entity

B. Measures taken to restrict or prohibit financial transactions with a country or entity

C. Measures taken to restrict or prohibit trade with a specific country or entity

D. Measures taken to isolate a country or entity diplomatically

Answer: C

What are the different types of sanctions?

A. Economic, social, political, and environmental

B. Trade, diplomatic, technological, and educational

C. Economic, trade, financial, diplomatic, and travel

D. Humanitarian, cultural, scientific, and sporting

Answer: C

What is the history of sanctions?

A. It dates back to the 20th century

B. It dates back to the Middle Ages

C. It dates back to ancient times

D. It dates back to the 18th century

Answer: C

What are travel sanctions?

A. Measures taken to restrict or prohibit trade with a specific country or entity

B. Measures taken to restrict or prohibit financial transactions with a country or entity

C. Measures taken to restrict or prohibit travel to a specific country or entity

D. Measures taken to isolate a country or entity

diplomatically

Answer: C

SANCTIONS EVASION

Sanctions evasion refers to the act of circumventing or violating sanctions imposed by governments or international organizations, often through deceptive or illegal means. Sanction evasion can take various forms, such as hiding the identity of sanctioned entities, using front companies or intermediaries, engaging in trade-based money laundering, or exploiting loopholes in the sanctions regime. Sanctions evasion is considered a serious offense and can result in severe legal and reputational consequences for individuals and organizations involved. Sanctions compliance programs aim to prevent, detect and mitigate the risk of sanction evasion.

SANCTION EVASION TECHNIQUES

Sanction Evasion Techniques are used by affected entities to circumvent economic sanctions. They are part of the broader concept of sanctions. The Office of Foreign Assets Control is the main US body that slaps sanctions on foreign countries, organizations and individuals. However, if the OFAC has put sanctions on countries like North Korea, Iran and Russia, how are these countries still able to partake in the trade of goods and move money outside of their borders?

Many individuals and organizations within the countries may be using banks and other financial institutions within the country to facilitate their illegal activities. Most of the time, these institutions do not even know the true purpose of these transactions. This can be extremely risky for them, as the consequences for not adhering to Sanction Evasion Techniques are very heavy.

So, what are the most common techniques these organizations use to evade sanctions and continue partaking in financial activities that are essential for their country's economic health? Direct violation and legal loopholes are commonly used techniques to evade sanctions.

Businesses in third-party states or in the sanctioning state may be willing to tolerate the risks of detection and punishment and engage in "sanctions-busting" on behalf of targeted entities. This can be very profitable, especially if the sanctions have significantly affected the targets' terms of trade.

TRADE TECHNIQUES

Blatant violation of sanctioned terms and penetrating the legal loopholes are the two commonly used techniques to evade trade sanctions. Businesses in third-party states or in the sanctioning state may be willing to tolerate the risks of detection and punishment and engage in "sanctions-busting" on behalf of targeted entities. This can be very profitable, especially if the sanctions have significantly affected the targets' terms of trade. Here are some tricks of trade techniques.

SMUGGLING

Smuggling is a common technique used by individuals and organizations to evade economic sanctions. The basic idea is to smuggle goods or currency across borders, bypassing legal channels and avoiding detection by authorities. Smuggling can be helpful in evading sanctions because it enables the flow of goods and money that would otherwise be blocked by sanctions.

One way that smuggling can be helpful in evading sanctions is by providing access to essential goods that are subject to sanctions, such as food, medicine, and energy supplies. When these goods are in short supply due to sanctions, smugglers can provide a source of supply to people who need them, even if they have to pay higher prices.

Another way that smuggling can be helpful in evading sanctions is by enabling access to goods or services that are subject to restrictions or embargoes.

For example, if a country is prohibited from importing a particular type of technology or equipment, smugglers may be able to bring it in illegally, enabling the country to acquire the technology or equipment it needs.

Smuggling can also be helpful in evading sanctions by providing a way to move money across borders. When sanctions block the flow of funds, smugglers can provide a means of transferring money without being detected.

For example, they may use cash couriers, hawala networks, or other informal channels to move funds.

However, it's important to note that smuggling is often illegal and can have negative consequences.

Smugglers may exploit vulnerable populations, engage in corrupt practices, or undermine legitimate economic activity.

Additionally, the use of smuggling to evade sanctions can exacerbate tensions and prolong conflict, making it more difficult to find a peaceful resolution.

BARTER TRADE

Barter trade, also known as countertrade, is a type of trade where goods and services are exchanged directly, without the use of money. Barter trade can be used as a method of evading sanctions because it can allow countries to acquire the goods they need without having to use the international financial system, which is typically subject to sanctions.

In the context of evading sanctions, barter trade frequently entails the exchange of non-sanctioned goods for sanctioned goods.

For example, a country subject to sanctions might exchange oil or other commodities for food, medicine, or other goods that are not subject to sanctions. This allows the country to acquire the goods it needs without using the international financial system or engaging in direct financial transactions with countries or entities that are subject to sanctions.

Barter trade can be difficult to monitor and regulate, making it a popular method of sanctions evasion. However, it can also be risky, as it can be difficult to ensure that both sides are receiving a fair exchange of goods and services. Additionally, barter trade can be limited by factors such as geographic proximity, trade imbalances, and differences in the types of goods and services that are needed by different countries.

RE-EXPORTING OF GOODS

Re-export is a technique that is commonly used to evade sanctions. This technique involves the use of a third-party country as a transit point for goods that are destined for a sanctioned country.

The re-export technique is used to circumvent the restrictions imposed by the sanctions by introducing a layer of anonymity between the exporter and the importer.

To execute the re-export technique, a company in a third-party country purchases goods from the exporter in the sanctioning country, and then sells them to a company in the sanctioned country. The goods are shipped from the sanctioning country to the third-party country, and then re-exported to the sanctioned country. This creates a loophole in the sanctions, which enables the exporter to conduct business with the sanctioned country, while appearing to comply with the rules.

Re-export can take many forms, including the trans-shipment of goods through multiple countries, the use of front companies to conceal the identity of the true exporter or importer, and the falsification of shipping and customs documents. The use of re-export is facilitated by the globalized nature of trade and the complexities of global supply chains.

The use of re-export to evade sanctions is illegal and can result in severe penalties. Countries with sanctions regimes in place have become increasingly vigilant in monitoring re-export activities to detect and prevent violations. However, the enforcement of sanctions can be challenging due to the complexity of global supply chains and the involvement of multiple stakeholders, including brokers, freight forwarders, and financial intermedaiaries.

In summary, the re-export technique is a common method used to evade sanctions, and it involves the use of a third-party country as a transit point for goods that are destined for a sanctioned country. The technique exploits the complexity of global trade and supply chains and is illegal and subject to penalties.

SHIPMENTS TO PORTS CLOSE TO SANCTIONED COUNTRIES

Using ports close to sanctioned countries is another technique for evading sanctions. This involves redirecting the flow of goods through ports in neighboring countries that are not subject to the same level of sanctions.

For instance, if a country has been sanctioned and cannot trade with other countries, it may opt to route its trade through a neighboring country that is not under sanctions. In this way, the sanctioned country can continue to conduct trade without directly violating sanctions.

This technique may require the use of intermediaries or front companies to obscure the true origin or destination of goods, making it difficult for authorities to track the movement of goods and enforce sanctions.

However, this technique can also be risky as authorities can closely monitor the movement of goods through neighbouring countries and may impose additional restrictions or sanctions on these countries to discourage them from facilitating sanctions evasion. Additionally, the use of intermediaries and front companies can expose businesses to the risk of sanctions violations and other legal consequences.

A prominent example is Dandong, China, which has been identified as a major transhipment point for goods being sent to North Korea in violation of the sanctions imposed by United Nations.

CREATING SHELL COMPANIES

This is probably the easiest and most common way for organizations to bypass sanctions. Criminals usually use shell companies as fronts for money laundering operations. When countries want to move funds from one country to another without detection, it is essentially a form of money laundering. They set up shell companies to transfer money to the sanctioned entities under the cover of anonymity. The sanctioned countries set up shell companies in quick succession. They each one for a short period of time for heavy activity, then closing them down and moving on to the next one.

Many countries actually use their government-operated businesses to open up these companies as branches in neighbouring countries to conduct their operations through.

These companies fool financial institutions into thinking they are legitimate companies. They then finance them and provide them with the means to transfer funds.

Hence, law enforcement advises that financial institutions must always conduct thorough due diligence on the companies they provide funds to. In doing so, they may be able to trace the company's actions back to the ultimate patron. The source may very well end up being a sanctioned individual or entity.

Some details financial institutions must look out for when screening potential shell companies are their registered address, whether they have any legitimate online presence and common directors across a network of companies. If the address of the company is in a tax haven area or area bordering a heavily sanctioned country, has zero online presence when searched for and has persons with political affiliations on its board of directors, then it counts as a red flag.

AIS RECORD ALTERATIONS

AIS (Automatic Identification System) is a tracking system used for maritime navigation and collision avoidance. Vessels equipped with AIS regularly broadcast their identity, position, speed, and course to other vessels and shore-based stations.

This system can be used to monitor vessels' movements and activities, including those involved in trade with countries subject to sanctions. One technique used to evade sanctions is the alteration of AIS records. This involves manipulating the information transmitted by the AIS system to hide the vessel's true identity or destination. AIS operates by sending out digital signals from a vessel's transponder, which are then received by other vessels and by shore-based stations. The signals include information about the vessel's identity, such as its name and call sign, as well as its location, course, and speed. This information is displayed on electronic chart displays, allowing operators to track the movements of vessels in real-time.

For example, a vessel that is engaged in trade with a sanctioned country might change its AIS destination to a non-sanctioned country, making it appear as though it is engaged in legitimate trade.

AIS alteration can be achieved through the use of various technologies, including GPS signal jammers, AIS signal blockers, and AIS signal simulators. These technologies can be used to mask the vessel's true location or create false AIS signals to misrepresent the vessel's identity or destination.

Here are three most popular techniques of alteration of the AIS records.

- Switching off the AIS: The most straightforward way to alter AIS is simply to turn it off. This can be done manually by the crew of a vessel, or it can be done automatically if the AIS system fails or loses power. Vessels may choose to turn off their AIS for a variety of reasons, such as to avoid detection by authorities, to prevent piracy or hijacking, or to preserve their privacy.

- Spoofing the AIS: Another way to alter AIS is to spoof the signals that are sent out by a vessel's transponder. This involves sending out false information about the vessel's identity, location, course, or speed. Spoofing can be done using specialized equipment, and it can be used to make a vessel appear to be in a different location or to have a different identity than it actually has.

- Tampering with the AIS: AIS can also be altered by physically tampering with the transponder or its antenna. This can involve removing or damaging the transponder, or interfering with the signal that it sends out. Tampering with AIS can be more difficult to detect than simply turning it off or spoofing it, and it may require physical inspection of the vessel to uncover. However, it is also a risky technique, as it can be detected through the use of other surveillance technologies, such as satellite imagery or radar. Additionally, many countries have laws that prohibit the alteration of AIS records, and violators can face significant penalties.

ALTERATION OF IMO

IMO plays a key role in implementing and enforcing sanctions measures that target the shipping industry. IMO works closely with other international organizations, such as the United Nations Security Council and the European Union, to develop and implement sanctions regimes that target vessels and shipping companies that are suspected of engaging in illegal activities or violating sanctions.

For example, IMO maintains a database of all vessels that are subject to United Nations sanctions, and it provides information to member states and other organizations about these vessels and their owners. IMO also works to raise awareness among the shipping industry about the risks and consequences of sanctions violations, and it provides guidance to ship owners and operators on how to comply with sanctions measures.

Vessels are required to display their name and IMO number in a visible location, which allows for their identification and tracking. The IMO number is a unique seven-digit number that is assigned to a vessel at the time of its construction, and it is intended to be permanent regardless of changes in ownership or name.

However, sanctions evaders may attempt to obscure or manipulate the IMO number to evade detection and disguise the connection of the vessel to a country subject to sanctions. For example, they may paint over or remove the IMO number from the vessel's hull, or they may change the number illegally to make it appear as if the vessel is registered in a different country or under a different name.

These actions can make it more difficult for authorities to identify and track vessels that are subject to sanctions, and they may require additional investigation and intelligence-gathering to uncover.

Additionally, a ship or shipping company may provide false or misleading information to the IMO or other authorities about their ownership, operations, or activities. For example, they may provide false documents or invoices to conceal their involvement in prohibited activities, or they may claim that their cargo is destined for a different port or country in order to avoid detection.

TRANSSHIPMENTS

Transshipment is the transfer of goods or cargo from one vessel to another while in transit. This can occur at sea or in a port, and it is typically done to transfer cargo between vessels that are traveling different routes or to consolidate cargo from multiple vessels onto a single vessel for more efficient transportation.

Transshipment can be a legitimate business practice and can offer benefits such as cost savings and faster transit times. However, it can also be used for illicit purposes, such as to evade sanctions, customs duties, or other regulations. For example, a sanctioned entity may use transshipment to move goods from one vessel to another in order to conceal the origin or destination of the goods and avoid detection by authorities.

Transshipment can be used to evade sanctions by allowing sanctioned entities to move goods between multiple vessels, ports, and countries in order to avoid detection by authorities. For example, a sanctioned entity may use transshipment to move goods from a sanctioned country to a third country without directly transporting them through a port that is subject to sanctions.

Transshipment can also be used to disguise the origin or destination of goods, which can make it more difficult for authorities to enforce sanctions. A sanctioned entity may use transshipment to mix sanctioned goods with non-sanctioned goods or to alter the packaging or labelling of goods in order to hide their true contents.

In addition, transshipment can allow sanctioned entities to use intermediary companies and vessels to carry out prohibited activities. For example, a sanctioned entity may use a shell company or intermediary vessel to conduct transactions or to transport goods, which can make it more difficult for authorities to trace the activities back to the sanctioned entity.

Transshipment can be difficult to monitor and regulate, as it often involves multiple vessels and parties, and cargo may be transferred multiple times before reaching its final destination.

CHANGING THE FLAGS STATE

Flag state refers to the country under whose flag a ship or vessel is registered and operates. The flag state has certain responsibilities and obligations with respect to the vessel and its operations, including regulating its safety and environmental performance, ensuring compliance with international laws and regulations, and overseeing the certification and training of its crew.

The choice of flag state can have important implications for a vessel or shipping company, as it can affect the vessel's regulatory requirements, liability, and access to certain ports and shipping lanes. Some countries are known for having more lenient regulatory regimes, and vessels may choose to register under their flag in order to take advantage of this.

However, the choice of flag state can also have reputational implications, as some flag states may be associated with lower safety standards, environmental protection, or labor rights. This can impact a vessel's ability to secure business or to access certain ports or customers that prioritize these concerns.

In the context of sanctions, flag state can also be relevant, as vessels registered under the flag of a sanctioned country may be subject to additional restrictions or prohibitions on their operations and movements. For example, a vessel owned by a company that is subject to sanctions may change its name and flag state to that of a different country that is not subject to sanctions. By doing this, the vessel may be able to continue operating and conducting business without being detected by authorities.

USING TRADE FINANCE VEHICLES

Entities may use trade finance vehicles like ships and aircraft to facilitate the movement of funds and other goods across borders. Trade Finance Vehicles refer to those vehicles that help make international trade and commerce possible. They have the authority to move across international borders either by land, air or sea.

Most entities use shipping links to move along the trade of laundered money or transport goods from their country to another. These activities may not be possible normally due to sanctions.

They also provide manipulated or falsified documentation and pay off shipping agencies. This helps make it look like the transports are legitimate. In fact, these documents help to create an intricate paper trail. It is extremely difficult for involved financial institutions to follow and prove the original purpose of the shipment. Financial institutions usually grant funds and loans to shipments based on documents. So, providing documents indistinguaishable from legitimate documents make it easy for sanctioned entities to receive safe passage.

Russia and North Korea are regular offenders when it comes to using Trade Finance Vehicles for evading sanctions.

Financial institutions would be advised to keep these red flags in mind when approving transactions for cross-border shipments.

If a regular shipment appears to be much smaller or larger in quantity than expected.

- When official documents show discrepancies regarding the value and volume of the shipment. They do not match after inspection of the shipment.

- If the shipments take long detours or pass through countries that are not related to the nature of the shipment. This is especially suspicious if the countries the goods pass through are known for being at high risk of being illicit trade finance vehicles.

- If the products themselves are considered to be at high risk for trade-based money laundering and similar activities. This includes goods like alcohol, cigarettes, clothes, edible products etc. This usually includes goods that individually are low in cost, but are transported in large numbers at a time.

- When organizations pay for large shipments in cash, it throws up a lot of red flags. Launderers usually dispose of illegally obtained cash using such methods.

- If the payment is provided for by individuals or companies who do not seem related to the nature of goods in the shipment, then it may raise some concerns.

Governmental bodies may put sanctions on offending countries to show their disapproval of their actions. However, the sanctioned countries do not always follow these restrictions. Sanction Evasion Techniques play an important role in sanctions.

Many sanctioned countries like Iran, North Korea and Russia are still very much present in international trade. This is thanks to ingenious methods that make their activities difficult to detect. Unfortunately, they often rope in unsuspecting financial institutions, which face the brunt of the consequences when these activities are detected.

Countries and organizations will always keep coming up with innovative methods to bypass sanctions. Hence, it is up to financial institutions and the attached law enforcement entities to keep up with these methods. They must always perform adequate screening.

FINANCIAL TECHNIQUES

The financial technique of sanction evasion refers to the strategies and methods employed by individuals, entities, or even countries to bypass or circumvent economic sanctions imposed by governments or international bodies. Sanctions are measures imposed to restrict or prohibit certain financial transactions, trade activities, or interactions with targeted individuals, organizations, or nations, typically as a response to their involvement in illegal activities, human rights violations, or threats to international peace and security.

USE OF THE ALTERNATIVE CURRENCIES

The use of alternative currencies is one of the techniques that can be used to evade sanctions. Sanctions often restrict access to major global financial networks, such as SWIFT (Society for Worldwide Interbank Financial Telecommunication), which limits the ability of sanctioned entities to conduct international transactions in traditional currencies such as the US dollar or the euro.

In this context, the use of alternative currencies such as bitcoin and other cryptocurrencies, as well as bartering, can be used to facilitate transactions between sanctioned entities and their business partners. These alternative currencies can be used to transfer value outside of traditional financial channels, allowing for more anonymous and less traceable transactions that can evade sanctions.

However, the use of cryptocurrencies for sanctions evasion has its own challenges. Cryptocurrencies are still relatively new and not yet widely accepted by mainstream businesses, which can limit their usefulness for large-scale commercial transactions. Additionally, the high volatility of cryptocurrency values can make transactions risky, and their decentralized nature can make them more difficult to regulate and monitor.

Despite these challenges, the use of alternative currencies for sanctions evasion is a growing concern for global policymakers and enforcement agencies. As such, they are working to develop regulatory frameworks to address these challenges and prevent the use of these currencies for illegal purposes.

USING CORRESPONDENT BANKS

Correspondent banks refer to banks and financial institutions that offer services to other banks. This usually includes institutions in other countries. Countries looking to evade sanctions may conduct their activities through these banks to make sure their funds cross international borders. Sanctioned entities or governments create accounts in the name of various corporates in foreign countries.

Correspondence banks usually do not probe much into the activities of corporate accounts, which decreases the level of security applied to their transactions. This helps sanctioned entities perform activities without detection, through the means of US dollars.

Using dollars helps to repel suspicion as well. Large transactions made in the sanctioned country's currency are bound to attract attention. With the use of corporate accounts, entities and individuals are able to shield their real identities. They hide under the guise of a corporate entity. This diverts the attention of U.S. regulatory and financial institutions away from them.

In this case, monitoring the area of jurisdiction of the corporate behind the bank account may prove to be useful in identifying sanctioned entities.

COVER PAYMENTS

Cover payments refer to a financial technique used by banks to conceal the involvement of sanctioned entities in transactions that would otherwise be prohibited by sanctions laws.

Under sanctions regulations, transactions with certain countries, entities, and individuals are prohibited or subject to strict restrictions. When banks want to conduct a transaction that involves a sanctioned entity, they might use cover payments to conceal the identity of the sanctioned entity and make the transaction appear legitimate.

Cover payments involve making an additional payment, typically in a different currency and using a different bank, to obscure the identity of the sanctioned entity. For example, if a bank wanted to transfer funds to a sanctioned entity, it might use a third party to make the payment on its behalf, concealing the involvement of the sanctioned entity.

While cover payments are not necessarily illegal, they can be used to circumvent sanctions regulations and can be a red flag for potential sanctions violations. As a result, financial institutions must have robust compliance programs in place to screen transactions and customers for potential sanctions risks and prevent potential violations.

Let's say there is a company in Country A that is subject to international sanctions due to its involvement in illicit activities. The company wants to continue doing business with a company in Country B, which is not subject to sanctions. However, financial institutions closely monitor transactions involving the sanctioned company.

To evade the sanctions, the companies involved might engage in a cover payment scheme. They could set up a complex series of transactions where the sanctioned company pays an intermediary in Country B for seemingly legitimate goods or services. The intermediary, acting as a front, then makes a payment to the non-sanctioned company. The payment instructions and documentation are carefully crafted to make it appear as if the funds originated from legitimate sources and were unrelated to the sanctioned company.

By using cover payments, the sanctioned company can effectively mask its involvement in the transaction and evade detection by authorities and financial institutions monitoring for sanctions compliance. This allows them to continue conducting business and accessing financial services despite being subject to sanctions.

SWIFT STRIPPING

Swift stripping is a technique used to evade sanctions that involves the removal of references to sanctioned individuals or entities from financial transactions. This is done by removing information about the parties involved in the transaction or by providing misleading information that obscures the true nature of the transaction.

The Society for Worldwide Interbank Financial Telecommunication (SWIFT) is the primary messaging system used by banks and financial institutions to transfer money and communicate information about financial transactions. When a transaction is processed through SWIFT, it includes information about the sender and receiver of the funds, as well as details about the purpose of the transaction and any associated parties[ii].

In order to evade sanctions, individuals and entities may attempt to remove references to sanctioned parties from the SWIFT message or provide false information about the nature of the transaction. This can be done by using aliases or shell companies to disguise the true identity of the parties involved.

Swift stripping can be difficult to detect, as it requires close scrutiny of financial records and the ability to link related transactions. However, banks and financial institutions are required to maintain records of all financial transactions, and may be subject to fines or other penalties for engaging in sanctions evasion. There are multiple instances where the SWIFT messages have been tampered in past. In some cases financial institution may deliberately remove or alter information related to sanctioned individuals or entities in SWIFT messages to hide their involvement in a transaction. By disguising the true beneficiaries or counterparties, they aim to avoid triggering sanctions-related alerts or scrutiny.

SWIFT messages can also be manipulated to misrepresent the nature or purpose of a transaction. For instance, the details may be altered to make a payment appear as a legitimate business transaction when it is, in fact, related to sanctioned activities.

REPEATED SUBMISSION OF TRANSACTION

Resubmission of rejected transactions is a technique of sanctions evasion that involves repeatedly submitting financial transactions that have been rejected due to sanctions compliance concerns. This is done in the hope that the transaction will eventually be processed, as the sheer volume of transactions can make it difficult for banks to catch and stop every violation.

To evade detection, sanctions evaders may also attempt to disguise the true nature of transactions by altering the amounts, dates, and beneficiaries of transactions, or by using shell companies and intermediaries to obscure the true parties involved. Resubmitting rejected transactions and other techniques for evading sanctions can be illegal and carry significant penalties, including fines and imprisonment.

It can also damage a company's reputation and lead to the loss of business and banking relationships.

SUSPENSE ACCOUNTS

A suspense account is typically used by financial institutions to temporarily hold funds when there is uncertainty about their proper allocation. Suspense accounts can be used to evade sanctions by creating a layer of obscurity around the transactions. A suspense account is a temporary account that holds funds until a final destination account can be determined. This technique can be used to disguise the true destination of funds and avoid detection by financial institutions that monitor transactions for potential sanctions violations.

For example, a company could use a suspense account to hold funds intended for a sanctioned entity. The company would then transfer the funds to a non-sanctioned entity, but report the transfer as going to a different non-sanctioned entity. The transfer would appear legitimate, but in reality, the sanctioned entity would receive the funds from the non-sanctioned entity.

Suspense accounts are often used in combination with other evasion techniques, such as altering AIS records or using shell companies to further obscure the transaction. The use of suspense accounts can be difficult to detect, as it may appear as a legitimate transaction, and the account may be held at a reputable financial institution. However, regulators and law enforcement agencies are becoming increasingly aware of the use of suspense accounts in sanctions evasion and are implementing measures to detect and prevent their use.

One example of a suspense account being used in sanctions evasion involves a company called Lloyds Bank. In 2009, Lloyds Bank was fined $350 million by the United States government for violating U.S. sanctions against Iran, Sudan, and other countries. The bank was found to have used a "suspense account" to hide the identities of the entities involved in these transactions.

The transactions were processed through the bank's New York branch, which meant that they were subject to U.S. sanctions regulations. However, Lloyds Bank employees altered the names of the companies involved in these transactions in order to avoid detection. The altered names were then used to create "suspense accounts" that concealed the true identities of the entities involved.

The use of suspense accounts allowed Lloyds Bank to process transactions that would have otherwise been blocked by U.S. sanctions. The bank's actions were discovered during a U.S. government investigation, and Lloyds Bank ultimately paid a large fine for its role in the sanctions evasion scheme.

By funneling funds through the suspense account, banks create a layer of opacity and complexity that makes it challenging for regulatory authorities to trace the origin and destination of the funds. This allows banks to mask the involvement of sanctioned entities and obscure the true nature of the transactions. Instead of directly transferring funds to or from sanctioned entities, banks utilize the suspense account as an intermediary step, effectively obfuscating the flow of funds.

SPECIAL PURPOSE FINANCIAL STRUCTURES

Special Purpose Entities (SPEs), also known as shell companies, are a common method used for sanctions evasion. SPEs are legal entities that are created for a specific purpose, often to hold assets or conduct a specific business activity. They are typically created in jurisdictions with less stringent financial regulations or in offshore tax havens.

SPEs can be used to conceal the true ownership of assets or transactions, which makes them attractive for sanctions evasion. For example, an individual or company subject to sanctions may use an SPE to conduct transactions that would otherwise be prohibited. The SPE may also be used to hold assets that are subject to sanctions, such as oil or gas fields in a sanctioned country.

In some cases, SPEs may also be used to facilitate the re-export of goods to a sanctioned country. For example, an SPE located in a third country may purchase goods from a non-sanctioned country and then re-export them to the sanctioned country, bypassing the sanctions.

SPEs can also be used to launder money and hide illicit funds. By creating a network of SPEs in different jurisdictions, it is possible to move funds around and make it difficult to trace the source of the funds.

Examples of companies that have used SPEs for sanctions evasion include the Iranian airline Mahan Air, which has been sanctioned by the US and EU for its support of the Iranian government's nuclear and missile programs. The company reportedly used a network of front companies and shell companies to evade sanctions and purchase aircraft and parts. Another example is the Russian energy company Rosneft, which was sanctioned by the US in 2014 for its involvement in the conflict in Ukraine. The company reportedly used SPEs to conceal its ownership of assets and continue to do business with western companies.

DISGUISED PAYMENTS

disguised payment refers to a deliberate attempt to conceal the true nature or purpose of a financial transaction in order to evade sanctions regulations. It involves manipulating the transaction details to make it appear as if the payment is legitimate and unrelated to sanctioned entities or prohibited activities.

There are several techniques used to disguise payments in sanctions evasion. One common method is the falsification of invoices or documentation associated with the transaction. This can involve altering the description of goods or services, misrepresenting the pricing, or creating fictitious invoices to make the payment appear as a legitimate business transaction. By manipulating the payment documentation, the true purpose of the transaction is concealed, allowing it to bypass sanctions scrutiny.

Another technique used in disguising payments is the misclassification of goods or services. This involves intentionally categorizing the transaction under a different industry or product code that is not subject to sanctions. By misclassifying the transaction, the parties involved attempt to create the impression that the payment is unrelated to sanctioned entities or activities, thereby avoiding detection.

Disguised payments can also involve the use of intermediaries or front companies to obscure the true identities of the parties involved. These intermediaries act as a cover, making it difficult for authorities to trace the payment back to the sanctioned entity or activity. By employing multiple layers of transactions or utilizing complex payment structures, the true beneficiaries and sources of the funds can be effectively concealed.

The purpose of disguised payments is to deceive regulators and enforcement agencies by making the transactions appear legitimate while circumventing sanctions. By disguising the true nature or purpose of the payment, individuals or entities involved in sanctioned activities seek to avoid detection, penalties, and other consequences associated with violating sanctions regulations.[iii].

For example, a company in a sanctioned country may use a third-party intermediary located in a non-sanctioned country to conduct transactions. The intermediary would then use a series of layered payments to move the funds through multiple banks and jurisdictions before ultimately reaching the intended recipient.

This technique can be effective in evading sanctions, as it makes it difficult for authorities to detect and track the flow of funds. However, it is also risky, as it requires the involvement of multiple intermediaries, each of whom could potentially be caught and prosecuted for sanctions violations.

While both cover payments and disguised payments are methods used in sanctions evasion, the key difference lies in their approach. Cover payments focus on concealing the involvement of sanctioned entities or activities, while disguised payments involve manipulating the transaction details to make them appear legitimate. Both methods are aimed at bypassing sanctions controls and avoiding detection, but they employ different strategies to achieve their objectives.

Practice Questions

What is AIS in the context of sanctions compliance?

A. A type of sanctions list

B. A tool used for tracking maritime vessels

C. A regulatory body that enforces sanctions

D. A type of financial transaction

Answer: B.

What is the purpose of an IMO number?

A. To indicate a vessel's ownership

B. To display a vessel's name

C. To identify a vessel's flag state

D. To uniquely identify a vessel

Answer: D.

How can transshipment be used to evade sanctions?

A. By shipping goods to a different port than originally intended

B. By using a different vessel to transport goods

C. By mixing sanctioned goods with non-sanctioned goods

D. All of the above

Answer: D.

What is a common technique used to evade financial sanctions?

A. Using front companies

B. Smuggling

C. Mislabeling or misrepresenting goods

D. Using cash or alternative currencies

Answer: D

What are front companies used for in relation to sanctions evasion?

A. To conduct transactions that are difficult to trace or monitor

B. To smuggle goods into a country

C. To mislabel or misrepresent goods

D. To conceal the true ownership or activities of an individual or entity

Answer: D

Chapter

3

THE EXTRATERRITORIALITY OF SANCTIONS

Sanctions are part of a governing body's foreign laws and policies. Countries usually impose sanctions on other countries. However, if a country's governing body is only in charge of its own territory and people, how can it impose laws on areas out of its jurisdiction? This ability is called extraterritoriality- when a government can impose laws on areas outside of its normal areas of jurisdiction.

EXTRATERRITORIALITY OF SANCTIONS

Extraterritoriality of sanctions refers to the application of a country's sanctions on non-U.S. persons, entities, or activities that take place outside of the United States. This means that the sanctions laws and regulations of a particular country, such as the United States, may apply to foreign individuals, entities, or activities that have no direct connection to the country's jurisdiction, but which may have an indirect connection to the country through their involvement in sanctioned transactions or activities. The concept of extraterritoriality is controversial, and it has been the subject of much debate and criticism from some foreign governments and businesses, who argue that it violates international law and can have unintended consequences on global trade and diplomatic relations. In normal cases, extraterritorial jurisdiction requires the cooperation of the second country. However, this is not the case with sanctions. Since the OFAC and OFSI view sanctions as punitive, their intent is to penalize the offending country for their actions.

In this case, the country is bound to be un-cooperative. Hence, the OFAC and OFSI utilize extraterritorial jurisdiction to impose sanctions on the country. It is mandatory for all other countries to follow these rules, or they will face penalties as well.[iv]

Most sanctions, like those approved by the EU Council or United Nations Security Council, are formed by intergovernmental bodies. This makes them more well-thought-out and reasonable. These organizations impose sanctions in an attempt to restrict wrong-doers from committing heinous acts that may affect international relations and harmony. These sanctions are not exactly punitive in nature. They are rather put in place to help amend relations between conflicting nations.

Major global powers such as the United States of America and China have initiated stringent sanctions within their jurisdictions to penalize perpetrators of war crimes, genocide, and other grave offenses.

THE COMPLEX INTERNATIONAL TRADE NETWORK

No country in this world is completely independent. Each country relies on other nations for goods and services. This especially includes those which they may be unable to grow or manufacture on their own.

For example, a country that is subject to sanctions may turn to other countries or entities that are not subject to the same sanctions in order to continue trading. This can result in a complex network of transactions involving multiple countries and intermediaries, which can make it difficult to trace the true origin and destination of goods and funds.

In addition, the use of front companies, shell corporations, and other opaque business structures can further complicate the trade network and make it more difficult to identify and enforce sanctions violations. This can create a situation where a single transaction may involve multiple jurisdictions and legal frameworks, which can make it challenging for sanctioning countries to effectively enforce their sanctions policies.

Moreover, the global nature of the financial system means that a single transaction can involve multiple banks, each of which may be subject to different regulations and laws. This can create a situation where a single transaction may be legal in one country but illegal in another, further complicating the international trade network and making it more difficult to enforce sanctions.

Overall, the complex international trade network that can arise in the wake of sanctions highlights the challenges involved in enforcing sanctions policies, and underscores the importance of international cooperation and coordination in addressing these challenges.

The peace and harmony of the world depend on co-dependence and international relations. The international trade network is an intricate web where countries have agreements with each other to import and export specific goods at stipulated prices.

Many times, superpower countries impose sanctions on an offending country without consulting all the countries involved. This not only affects the sanctioned countries but other third-party countries as well.

IMPACT OF SANCTIONS ON UNINVOLVED COUNTRIES

While sanctions are intended to impact the targeted country or individual, they can have unintended consequences for other countries as well. Here are a few ways in which sanctions can negatively affect uninvolved countries:

ECONOMIC EFFECTS

Sanctions can disrupt global trade and supply chains, affecting countries that do not have a direct relationship with the targeted country. Sanctions can drive up prices for essential goods, reduce access to raw materials, and destabilize financial markets, all of which can impact the economy of uninvolved countries.

- Disruption of trade: Sanctions can disrupt trade flows, causing delays and higher transaction costs for businesses in uninvolved countries that depend on trade with the sanctioned country. This can also lead to higher prices for consumers in the uninvolved countries.

- Increased competition: Sanctions can lead to a reduction in exports from the sanctioned country, which can create opportunities for other exporters to step in and capture market share. This increased competition can put pressure on businesses in uninvolved countries that are already struggling to compete in global markets.

- Financial spillovers: Sanctions can cause financial spillovers by disrupting the flow of capital across borders. For example, banks in uninvolved countries may be forced to cut ties with banks in the sanctioned country, which can limit access to finance for businesses in the uninvolved country.

- Reduced investment: Sanctions can deter foreign investment in the sanctioned country, which can have knock-on effects on uninvolved countries that are part of the same supply chain or have other economic ties to the sanctioned country. This can lead to reduced growth, job losses, and other negative economic impacts.

- Refugee flows: Sanctions can lead to a deterioration of economic conditions in the sanctioned country, which can prompt large numbers of people to flee and seek refuge in neighboring countries. This can place a strain on the resources and social fabric of these uninvolved countries, leading to a range of economic and social challenges.

POLITICAL EFFECTS

Sanctions can also create political tensions between countries, particularly if the targeted country has close relationships with an uninvolved country.

For example, if a country has close political or economic ties with a sanctioned country, the sanctions may put pressure on the relationship between the uninvolved country and the sanctioning countries.

In some cases, the uninvolved country may disagree with the sanctions and view them as unjust or politically motivated. This can lead to tensions between the uninvolved country and the sanctioning countries, and may even result in diplomatic or economic retaliation.

On the other hand, some uninvolved countries may view sanctions as an opportunity to expand their own economic or political influence. For example, if a sanctioned country is a major exporter of a certain commodity, an uninvolved country may be able to step in and fill the gap in the market, potentially gaining new customers and increasing their own economic power.

Overall, the political impact of sanctions on uninvolved countries is complex and can depend on a variety of factors, including the nature of the sanctions, the relationship between the uninvolved country and the sanctioned country, and the political motivations behind the sanctions

For instance, a country that relies heavily on a targeted country for energy may feel pressure to push back against sanctions, straining relationships with the sanctioning country.

SECURITY IMPACT

Sanctions can also create security risks for uninvolved countries. For instance, sanctions can cause an increase in illicit activities like smuggling and money laundering, which can increase the likelihood of corruption, crime, and terrorism.

Sanctions on a target country can have security implications for uninvolved countries, particularly those in the region. One possible security impact is the displacement of people from the target country, who may seek refuge in neighboring countries. This can put a strain on the resources and stability of those countries, potentially leading to political and social unrest.

In addition, sanctions can lead to the collapse of the target country's economy, which may result in an increase in crime, including smuggling, piracy, and terrorism. Criminal organizations and terrorist groups may take advantage of the chaos to exploit weak governance and carry out attacks. This can create security threats for uninvolved countries in the region and beyond.

Furthermore, sanctions can strain diplomatic relations between countries, particularly when the uninvolved country has close ties with the target country. This can lead to a breakdown in cooperation on security issues, such as counterterrorism and countering the proliferation of weapons of mass destruction.

HUMANITARIAN IMPACT

Sanctions can also have a negative impact on the humanitarian situation in the targeted country, which can in turn create a refugee crisis and burden neighboring countries with an influx of displaced people.

It is important to note that the impact of sanctions on uninvolved countries can vary depending on the specifics of the sanctions and the relationships between the countries involved. Sanctions are a complex tool that can have far-reaching consequences, and should be used with caution.

One example of where uninvolved countries were affected by sanctions is the case of the U.S. sanctions against Russia that were imposed in response to Russia's annexation of Crimea in 2014. These sanctions targeted a range of Russian industries, including finance, energy, and defense, and were designed to put pressure on the Russian economy and government.

However, because Russia is a major energy exporter, the sanctions had a spillover effect on other countries that relied on Russian energy exports, such as European countries. The sanctions disrupted global energy markets and led to higher prices for natural gas, which had a negative impact on some European economies.

In addition, the sanctions also affected some non-Russian companies that had business ties with Russia, leading to a decrease in their profits and stock prices. This, in turn, affected the investors in these companies, including those from uninvolved countries.

THE CONCENTRATION OF POWER

The concept of a single country having enough power to impose sanctions may have more negative consequences than positive ones. Though the sanctioned country is in fact in the wrong, it is still a part of the complex international trade network.

Putting sanctions on trade not only impacts the lives of innocent citizens in the country but other nations as well. Hence, many sanctions end up punishing innocent bystanders rather than the government officials who are actually in the wrong.

Concentration of power can be dangerous for a sanctioning country because it can lead to overreliance on a single policy tool, such as sanctions, and an overestimation of their effectiveness. This can result in the neglect of other tools and strategies, leading to a myopic foreign policy approach.

Additionally, the use of sanctions can have unintended consequences that harm the sanctioning country's own economic and political interests. For example, if a sanctioning country's economy is heavily dependent on trade with the target country, the imposition of sanctions can disrupt trade flows and lead to economic harm for the sanctioning country. Similarly, if the target country responds to sanctions with retaliatory measures, this can harm the sanctioning country's political and security interests.

The ability to impose sanctions is a very powerful one, and nations must learn to gauge when to use it. It is better to leave their implementation to inter-governmental entities, which only impose them with the discussion and consent of all countries involved. This will help implement them in a manner that causes minimum damage to the countries having ties with the felonious country.

One example of the negative consequences of concentration of power in a sanctioning country is the unilateral sanctions imposed by the United States on Iran. The US has significant economic power and influence, which has allowed it to pressure other countries to follow its lead in imposing sanctions on Iran. This concentration of power has led to a situation where many countries have had to comply with the US sanctions, even if they disagree with them or have legitimate trade and economic relationships with Iran.

Another example is the sanctions imposed by the European Union on Russia in response to the annexation of Crimea. The EU's strong economic power and influence has made it difficult for many companies and countries to continue doing business with Russia, leading to significant economic harm and political tensions. In this case, the concentration of power in the hands of the EU has led to negative consequences for both the sanctioned country and the countries affected by the sanctions.

BLOCKING STATUTES

Some countries may put forward blocking statutes if they disagree with the extent of the sanctions.

Blocking statutes are laws enacted by countries to counteract the extraterritorial effects of foreign laws, particularly in the context of international economic sanctions. These statutes are designed to protect the interests of the country enacting them and its businesses and citizens from the effects of foreign laws that could harm their interests.[v]

For example, a blocking statute may prohibit companies based in the country from complying with the extraterritorial application of U.S. sanctions on a particular country or entity. These statutes may include provisions that criminalize compliance with foreign laws and may impose penalties on companies or individuals that cooperate with foreign enforcement efforts.

Blocking statutes can create conflicts of law and jurisdictional challenges, as they seek to counteract the effects of foreign laws within a country's borders. They can also create challenges for companies that operate across borders, as they may be subject to conflicting legal requirements in different jurisdictions.

Countries which trade with the sanctioned country on a regular basis or are co-dependent on them usually enact these. Blocking statutes basically means refusing to follow foreign country rulings or they are imposed by other countries.

CHALLENGES CAUSED BY BLOCKING STATUTES

Blocking statutes can create several challenges for the sanctioning country and can potentially create a difficult situation for the sanctioning country. Here are some of the challenges faced by the sanctioning country

- Limiting the effectiveness of sanctions: Blocking statutes can undermine the effectiveness of sanctions by prohibiting companies from complying with them. This can make it more difficult to achieve the desired policy goals, such as putting pressure on a target country to change its behaviour.

- Creating legal conflicts: Blocking statutes can create legal conflicts between the sanctioning country and the countries that have enacted them. This can lead to diplomatic tensions and potentially harm bilateral relations.

- Discouraging foreign investment: Companies may be hesitant to invest in the sanctioning country if they face the risk of violating blocking statutes in their home country. This can reduce foreign investment and economic growth in the sanctioning country.

- Limiting access to information: Blocking statutes can make it more difficult for the sanctioning country to obtain information about transactions involving its targets. This can make it more difficult to track and enforce sanctions violations.

- Raising compliance costs: Companies may need to invest more resources to comply with both the sanctions imposed by the sanctioning country and the blocking statutes in their home country. This can increase compliance costs and reduce profitability.

Blocking statutes have been used by various countries as a response to extraterritorial sanctions.

HISTORICAL BLOCKING STATUTES

Blocking statutes are laws enacted by countries to counter the extraterritorial effects of foreign laws, especially those of the United States. These laws are designed to protect their citizens and companies from the impact of foreign sanctions or other restrictive measures.

Some of the notable blocking statutes include:

- The EU Blocking Statute[vi]: The European Union adopted the Blocking Statute in 1996 to counteract the effects of the United States' extraterritorial sanctions on Iran and Cuba. The statute prohibits EU companies from complying with extraterritorial sanctions and provides a legal basis for companies to recover damages caused by foreign sanctions.

- French Blocking Statute: In 1968, France enacted a law that prohibits French companies from complying with foreign sanctions, especially those imposed by the United States. The law provides criminal penalties for companies that violate the statute.

- German Blocking Statute: The German Foreign Trade and Payments Act (Außenwirtschaftsgesetz) prohibits German companies from complying with foreign sanctions that are not supported by the United Nations. The law provides for criminal penalties and fines for companies that violate the statute.

- Russian Blocking Statute: In 2018, Russia enacted a law that prohibits Russian companies from complying with foreign sanctions. The law provides for penalties, including fines and restrictions on imports from the countries that impose sanctions on Russia.

- Chinese Blocking Statute: In January 2021, China's Ministry of Commerce enacted a blocking statute that prohibits Chinese companies from complying with foreign laws that apply extraterritorial jurisdiction. The law provides for countermeasures against the countries that impose extraterritorial sanctions on China

CASE STUDY OF INDIA

India does not have a specific blocking statute that governs the effects of international sanctions on Indian companies. However, India has taken steps to protect its domestic companies from the impact of international sanctions, particularly those imposed by the United States.

In 2018, India's Ministry of Commerce and Industry issued a notification directing all Indian government departments to give preference to domestically manufactured goods and services in public procurement, with exceptions for goods and services not available in India. This move was seen as a way to protect Indian companies from the impact of US sanctions on countries such as Iran, which had been a major trading partner for India.

In addition, in 2019, the Reserve Bank of India (RBI) introduced a new payment mechanism for trade with Iran, known as the "Rupee Payment Mechanism." Under this mechanism, Indian companies could purchase Iranian oil in rupees, which were held in an account in an Indian bank. These rupees could then be used to pay Indian exporters for goods and services, effectively bypassing the US financial system and avoiding US sanctions.

Overall, while India does not have a specific blocking statute in place, the government has taken steps to protect Indian companies from the impact of international sanctions, particularly those imposed by the United States.

Hence, countries may submit pleas to intergovernmental bodies to block statutes if they feel that sanctions on another country will affect them negatively. This gives them the ability to bypass them and continue operations with the sanctioned country as normal.

Sanctions are policies and restrictions put in place to prevent offending countries from continuing their odious activities. However, in many cases, they may end up causing more harm than good. Many superpower countries have too much power in their hands, which they use to impose sanctions without consulting with other countries beforehand. This can affect bystander countries that are not directly involved in the wrongdoing but depend on the wrongful country for essential goods. These countries can apply to block statutes if needed, to protect their trading and economy. Hence, it is important to review and revise who can impose sanctions and on what level. This would help make sure that it does not cross its limits and negatively affect innocent countries and citizens.

Practice Questions

What is the extraterritoriality of sanctions?

A. The application of sanctions laws and regulations to foreign governments only

B. The application of sanctions laws and regulations to non-U.S. persons or activities that take place outside of the United States

C. The application of sanctions laws and regulations to U.S. persons or activities that take place outside of the United States

D. The application of sanctions laws and regulations to foreign companies only

Answer: B

How do complex international trade networks affect the extraterritoriality of sanctions?

A. They make it easier for companies to comply with sanctions laws and regulations

B. They have no impact on the extraterritoriality of sanctions

C. They can make it difficult for companies and individuals to comply with sanctions laws and regulations

D. They only affect U.S. companies and individuals, not foreign ones

Answer: C

What are some potential consequences of the extraterritoriality of sanctions on global trade and diplomatic relations?

A. Increased cooperation and collaboration between countries

C. Unintended consequences on foreign businesses and economies

B. Decreased competition in the global market

D. Enhanced transparency in international transactions

Answer: C

What can companies and individuals do to ensure compliance with extraterritorial sanctions regimes?

A. Ignore the laws and regulations and continue with business as usual

C. Conduct business only with U.S. companies and individuals

B. Seek expert advice and stay up-to-date on the latest developments in sanctions laws and regulations

D. Lobby the government to change the laws and regulations to their benefit

Answer: B

Chapter

4

CRYPTOCURRENCY AND SANCTIONS EVASION

Cryptocurrencies present a new challenge for regulators and law enforcement agencies trying to enforce sanctions. Cryptocurrencies offer an alternative means of transferring value that is outside the traditional financial system and not subject to the same level of regulatory oversight.

ROLE OF CRYPTO ASSETS IN SANCTIONS EVASION

Cryptocurrencies have been used in several cases of sanctions evasion due to their anonymous and decentralized nature. Sanctions target the financial transactions and assets of sanctioned individuals, entities, and countries. Individuals and entities subject to sanctions can use cryptocurrencies to evade sanctions by conducting transactions anonymously, avoiding detection by traditional financial institutions and regulatory bodies. They can also use peer-to-peer exchanges or offshore exchanges that do not comply with international regulations to trade cryptocurrencies.

METHODS OF SANCTION EVASIONS

Cryptocurrencies have emerged as a new tool for sanctions evasion due to their anonymity, decentralization, and global reach. Here are some ways in which cryptocurrencies are used for sanctions evasion:

PURCHASING GOODS AND SERVICES

Cryptocurrencies can be used to purchase goods and services online, enabling individuals and entities subject to sanctions to bypass traditional financial institutions. Sanctioned individuals or entities can use cryptocurrency to purchase goods and services from non-sanctioned businesses, thereby bypassing the restrictions placed on them.

Purchasing goods in crypto can potentially evade sanctions because the transactions can be conducted anonymously or pseudonymously, making it difficult to identify the parties involved. This anonymity can be further enhanced by using decentralized exchanges that do not require users to provide personal information or by using privacy-focused cryptocurrencies such as Monero.

For example, if a sanctioned country is unable to import certain goods due to restrictions imposed by the sanctions, individuals or entities within that country may try to purchase the same goods from foreign suppliers using cryptocurrency. By doing so, they can avoid the traditional financial system and its associated controls, making it difficult for authorities to detect and prevent such transactions.

One example is the case of Iran, which has been subject to US sanctions that limit its access to the global financial system. In response, Iran has increasingly turned to cryptocurrencies such as Bitcoin to bypass these restrictions and facilitate international trade.

Iranian companies have used Bitcoin and other cryptocurrencies to purchase goods such as electronics, computer parts, and even cars from foreign suppliers. These transactions can be conducted without the need for traditional banking channels, making them difficult to track and regulate.

MONEY LAUNDERING

Cryptocurrencies can be used to transfer funds anonymously, making them attractive for money laundering activities. where sanctioned entities or individuals can use cryptocurrencies to receive payments for their goods or services, and then launder these funds to make them appear as legitimate income. This can be achieved through various methods such as transferring the funds through multiple accounts and exchanges, converting them into different cryptocurrencies, or using anonymous wallets and addresses to conceal the source of the funds.

Some of the common crypto currency money laundering techniques used for evading sanctions are provided here in the next few sections.

CHAIN HOPPING

One common technique used for crypto currency laundering is called "chain hopping." This involves moving crypto currencies from one exchange to another in a chain of transactions to make it difficult to trace the source and destination of the funds. For example, if a country is subject to sanctions and cannot directly purchase goods or services from another country, it may use chain hopping to first exchange its local currency for a cryptocurrency such as Bitcoin, then transfer the Bitcoin to another cryptocurrency such as Monero, and then finally exchange the Monero for a different cryptocurrency or fiat currency. By using multiple blockchains and cryptocurrencies, it can be difficult for authorities to trace the flow of funds and identify the parties involved in the transactions.

However, it is important to note that chain hopping is not foolproof and can still be subject to detection by skilled investigators and regulatory bodies. Additionally, the use of such techniques may be illegal and could result in severe penalties if caught.

MIXING

Another technique is called "mixing" or "tumbling," which involves sending crypto currencies through a mixing service or platform that pools funds together and then redistribute them to new addresses, making it difficult to trace the origin of the funds.

This technique can be used to evade sanctions by using mixing services to obfuscate the origin and destination of funds involved in a transaction. For example, an entity or individual subject to sanctions may use a mixing service to send crypto to a third party who is not subject to sanctions. The third party can then send the mixed crypto back to the original entity, effectively bypassing the sanctions.

PEELING CHAIN

Another method is called "peeling chains," where a person or entity sells a small amount of crypto currencies for a profit on one exchange, and then sells the same crypto currencies for a loss on another exchange, which appears to be a legitimate loss on the books. In a typical peeling chain transaction, a large amount of illicit funds is mixed with a much larger amount of legitimate funds, making it difficult to trace the illicit funds through the transaction chain. The mixed funds are then transferred through a series of transactions, each involving a smaller and smaller proportion of the original mixed funds, until the illicit funds are eventually separated from the legitimate funds and withdrawn or converted to another form of currency.

The use of peeling chain in crypto currency laundering for sanctions evasion involves setting up multiple accounts or wallets, and transferring funds back and forth between them in a complex network of transactions. The complexity of the transactions makes it difficult to trace the source of the funds or identify the individuals or entities involved in the transactions.

MICRO LAUNDERING

Micro laundering is a technique used to transfer small amounts of money from one account to another, making it difficult to detect and trace. In the context of sanctions evasion, micro laundering can be used to move small amounts of cryptocurrency through multiple accounts or exchanges to avoid detection.

For example, a person could use a cryptocurrency exchange to buy a small amount of a less popular cryptocurrency, then transfer that cryptocurrency to another exchange and sell it for a different cryptocurrency. This process could be repeated multiple times with small amounts of cryptocurrency, making it difficult for authorities to trace the original source and destination of the funds.

FACILITATING ILLEGAL ACTIVITIES

When it comes to sanctions evasion, some of the specific illegal activities that can be facilitated by crypto currencies include:

- Black market trading: Crypto currencies can be used to facilitate black market trading of goods and services that are prohibited by sanctions.
- Cybercrime: Crypto currencies can be used to facilitate cybercrime activities, such as hacking and ransomware attacks, which can be used to steal sensitive data or funds to evade sanctions.
- Fraud: Crypto currencies can be used to facilitate fraudulent activities, such as phishing scams, Ponzi schemes, and other financial frauds, which can be used to obtain funds to evade sanctions.
- Smuggling: Crypto currencies can be used to facilitate the payment for goods that are smuggled across borders to evade sanctions.

Two Iranian Nationals, Ali Khorashadizadeh and Mohammad Ghorbaniyan were accused of facilitating transactions related to the SamSam ransomware attacks, converting over 7,000 bitcoin transactions into Iranian rials and depositing them into Iranian banks. [vii]

OPERATING UNREGULATED EXCHANGES

Operating unregulated crypto exchanges is one way that can be used to facilitate sanctions evasion. These exchanges can provide a means for those subject to sanctions to convert their cryptocurrency into fiat currency or other forms of cryptocurrency without being subject to regulatory oversight.

By using unregulated exchanges, individuals or entities can transfer funds with a higher degree of anonymity, making it difficult for authorities to identify and prevent sanctions evasion. In addition, unregulated exchanges may not have proper know-your-customer (KYC) and anti-money laundering (AML) procedures in place, which can make it easier for sanctioned individuals or entities to use them for their transactions.

Furthermore, unregulated exchanges may not have proper security measures in place to prevent hacking, which could result in the theft of funds or private information. This could be particularly problematic if a sanctioned individual or entity is using an unregulated exchange to transfer funds that have been obtained illegally or through criminal activity.

To address this issue, regulators have begun to crack down on unregulated exchanges and impose stricter requirements for KYC and AML compliance. However, it remains a challenge to detect and prevent sanctions evasion through unregulated exchanges, particularly as the use of cryptocurrencies continues to grow in popularity.

In March 2021, a report by the United Nations Panel of Experts on North Korea revealed that the country had used a Hong Kong-based cryptocurrency exchange named "Global Digital" to launder over $100 million worth of stolen cryptocurrencies. The report also mentioned another exchange called "WMD Portal," which is believed to have links to North Korean hacking groups.

Another instance of North Korea's use of unregulated exchanges was revealed in 2019 when two Chinese nationals were indicted by the US Department of Justice for running an unlicensed money transmitting business that helped North Korea launder over $100 million in cryptocurrency.

OFAC ACTIONS

In December 2020, BitGo was fined by OFAC for failing to prevent individuals in sanctioned countries from opening accounts and sending digital currencies via its platform, resulting in 183 apparent violations[viii]. BitGo settled for $93,830. OFAC notes that BitGo had reason to know that these users were located in sanctioned jurisdictions based on IP data collected.

Similarly, in February 2021, OFAC entered into a $507,000 settlement with BitPay for allowing persons from sanctioned jurisdictions to transact with merchants in the US using crypto from its platform. BitPay failed to screen location data about its merchants' buyers resulting in 2,102 transactions on behalf of individuals located in sanctioned jurisdictions. These two enforcement actions highlight the importance of screening IP data to prevent VASPs from facilitating sanctioned transactions.

HIDING OWNERSHIP

Hiding ownership using cryptocurrencies can be used to evade sanctions by obscuring the true identity of the individuals or entities involved in the transaction. This can be done by using anonymous or pseudonymous cryptocurrency wallets or by transferring cryptocurrencies through a series of transactions to obfuscate the original source and destination.

For example, an individual or entity subject to sanctions may use a pseudonymous cryptocurrency wallet to transfer cryptocurrencies to a third party who is not subject to sanctions. The third party can then convert the cryptocurrencies into fiat currency or purchase goods on behalf of the sanctioned entity without triggering any sanctions violations.

Another method is to use shell companies or offshore accounts to hide ownership of cryptocurrencies. This can be done by registering a shell company in a jurisdiction with lax regulations or creating a cryptocurrency wallet in the name of an offshore entity. The sanctioned entity can then transfer cryptocurrencies to the shell company or offshore account, effectively hiding the true ownership of the funds.

ROLE OF PRIVACY COINS

Privacy-focused cryptocurrencies, such as Monero and Zcash, can be used in sanctions evasion to help conceal the identity of the sender and receiver of funds, as well as the origin and destination of the funds. Here are some ways in which privacy-focused cryptocurrencies can be used in sanctions evasion:

- Hiding transaction details: Privacy-focused cryptocurrencies use advanced cryptographic techniques to ensure that transactions are private and untraceable. This means that transaction details, such as the amount of funds transferred and the sender and receiver of funds, are not publicly visible on the blockchain. This makes it difficult for authorities to trace the flow of funds to and from sanctioned countries.

- Concealing wallet addresses: Privacy-focused cryptocurrencies allow users to generate new wallet addresses for each transaction. This means that the sender and receiver of funds are not linked to a specific wallet address, making it difficult for authorities to track the flow of funds.

- Avoiding detection: Privacy-focused cryptocurrencies can be used to avoid detection by authorities. For example, a user can use a privacy-focused cryptocurrency to transfer funds to a cryptocurrency exchange in a non-sanctioned country, convert the funds into a different cryptocurrency, and then transfer the funds to a wallet address in a sanctioned country. This can help to avoid detection by authorities who are monitoring traditional financial channels.

- Circumventing blockchain analysis: Privacy-focused cryptocurrencies can be used to circumvent blockchain analysis, which is a technique used by authorities to trace the flow of funds on the blockchain. Because transaction details are not publicly visible on the blockchain, authorities may have difficulty in tracing the flow of funds to and from sanctioned countries.

MITIGATING THE RISKS

Mitigating the risk associated with crypto currency sanction evasion techniques involves a combination of measures that can be taken by both governments and financial institutions. Some of these measures include:

Enhanced KYC/AML procedures: Financial institutions should implement more robust KYC and AML procedures that can detect unusual transactions involving crypto currencies. This includes screening for high-risk customers, conducting enhanced due diligence on transactions involving sanctioned entities, and monitoring transactions for unusual patterns.

Cooperation with regulatory authorities: Financial institutions should work closely with regulatory authorities and law enforcement agencies to share information on suspicious transactions and to help identify potential sanction evaders.

Training and awareness: Financial institutions should provide training to their staff on the risks associated with crypto currency transactions and how to detect and report suspicious activity.

Use of blockchain analysis tools: Blockchain analysis tools can be used to trace the flow of crypto currency transactions and to identify suspicious activity.

Compliance with international standards: Financial institutions should comply with international standards such as the FATF Recommendations and the Wolfsberg Group's guidance on virtual assets to ensure they are adequately addressing the risks associated with crypto currencies.

Sanctions screening software: Financial institutions can use sanctions screening software to ensure that they are not transacting with entities on a sanctions list.

Due diligence on crypto currency exchanges: Financial institutions should conduct due diligence on crypto currency exchanges they deal with to ensure they are reputable and have appropriate AML controls in place.

Overall, it is important for financial institutions to remain vigilant and continuously review and update their AML policies and procedures to address the evolving risks associated with crypto currencies and sanctions evasion.

Practice Questions

Which of the following is a way in which cryptocurrencies can be used to evade sanctions?

A. Purchasing goods through traditional banking channels

B. Laundering money through traditional financial institutions

C. Transferring funds through traditional payment networks

D. Purchasing goods on the dark web

Answer: D

What is the advantage of using privacy-focused cryptocurrencies in sanctions evasion?

A. They are faster and cheaper than traditional payment networks

B. They are backed by a government or central authority

C. They are subject to less regulatory scrutiny than traditional financial institutions

D. They can help conceal the identity of the sender and receiver of funds

Answer: D

How can privacy-focused cryptocurrencies help to avoid detection by authorities?

A. By generating new wallet addresses for each transaction

B. By linking the sender and receiver of funds to a specific wallet address

C. By making transaction details publicly visible on the blockchain

D. By requiring users to provide personal identification information

Answer: A

What is the disadvantage of using cryptocurrencies in sanctions evasion?

A. They are subject to heavy regulation and scrutiny by authorities

B. They are slower and more expensive than traditional payment networks

C. They are not widely accepted as a form of payment

D. They are not foolproof and can still be subject to detection and enforcement measures

Answer: D

SANCTION RISK

Sanctions risk for financial institutions refers to the potential negative consequences that a financial institution may face due to its involvement in activities that violate sanctions laws and regulations. This can include providing financial services to individuals, entities, or countries that are subject to sanctions, as well as failing to comply with sanctions laws and regulations.

SANCTION SCREENING

The risks associated with sanctions violations can be severe and can include financial penalties, reputational damage, legal action, loss of business, and in extreme cases, the loss of a financial institution's license to operate. Therefore, financial institutions must have robust compliance programs in place to prevent, detect, and report potential sanctions violations. These compliance programs should include policies and procedures, risk assessments, employee training, and ongoing monitoring and testing to ensure that the institution is effectively managing sanctions risk.

Sanction Risk Assessment is a key regulatory expectation; however, it is not a regulatory requirement. Sanction Risk is defined as direct exposure to embargoed jurisdictions or entities included on various sanction lists.

Failing to identify and comply with sanction rules can lead to financial penalties, freezing of assets and even criminal proceedings. This may apply to the sanctioned country, as well as the entities dealing with them.

Hence, the financial institution should identify the applicable sanctions-related regulations and understand their requirements. This includes not only the primary sanctions programs but also any secondary sanctions that could impact the institution's operations.

WHAT IS SANCTION SCREENING?

Sanctions screening is a process used by financial institutions and other companies to ensure compliance with sanctions regulations. It involves screening clients, transactions, and activities against various sanctions lists and other relevant databases to identify any prohibited or sanctioned individuals, entities, countries, or activities.

Sanctions screening typically involves the use of software that automatically compares the information from various sources against the relevant sanctions lists. This process helps companies identify any potential sanctions risks, and take appropriate action to prevent any violations.

The screening process can also include periodic reviews of clients, transactions, and activities to ensure that there are no changes that may impact sanctions compliance. This is important to ensure that companies are able to quickly identify and address any new risks that may emerge. The objective of sanctions screening is to identify any matches or potential matches between the screened data and the designated lists. Sanctions screening is a critical component of a financial institution's sanctions compliance program, as it helps prevent the institution from inadvertently processing transactions that violate sanctions regulations.

TYPES OF SANCTION SCREENINGS

There are two main types of sanctions risk screening:

- Bulk Screening: Bulk screening is the process of screening a large number of customers or transactions in a short period of time. This is typically done using an automated system that checks names against various sanctions lists. Bulk screening is useful for identifying potential sanctions risks quickly and efficiently.

- Triggered Screening: Triggered screening is the process of screening customers or transactions that have been flagged as potential sanctions risks. This may be due to a change in customer information, a change in the nature of a transaction, or other factors that could increase the risk of sanctions violations. Triggered screening is typically done manually and requires a higher level of scrutiny than bulk screening

It is essential to stay up-to-date with sanctions-related developments and changes in sanctions regulations. This includes monitoring sanctions lists and changes to them, as well as any sanctions-related news or updates from regulatory bodies.

WHY SANCTIONS SCREENING IS NECESSARY?

Keeping up with sanctioned entities is becoming more and more complex every day. Inter-governmental authorities update Sanction Risk lists quite regularly, with financial crimes and money laundering on the rise. Furthermore, many sanctioned countries, especially countries like North Korea and Russia, are finding new ways to evade economic sanctions and trade normally despite their wrong-doings[ix].

Sanctions screening is necessary for several reasons, including:

- Compliance with regulatory requirements: Financial institutions are required by law to comply with sanctions regulations, which are designed to prevent money laundering and terrorist financing. Sanctions screening is one of the key components of sanctions compliance.

- Risk management: Sanctions screening helps financial institutions to manage the risks associated with doing business with sanctioned individuals, entities, and countries. By identifying and blocking transactions involving sanctioned parties, financial institutions can reduce the risk of regulatory penalties, fines, and reputational damage.

- Protecting the financial system: Sanctions screening helps to protect the integrity of the financial system by preventing sanctioned parties from using it to move funds, finance illicit activities, or evade sanctions.

- Preventing criminal activity: Sanctions screening can help to prevent criminal activity, including money laundering, terror financing, and the proliferation of weapons of mass destruction.

Hence, it is up to banks and other FIs at the international level to ensure that their sanction screening procedures are up to date. Non-compliance with sanctions is punishable by law, but in some cases so is dealing with sanctioned entities. Adhering to sanction lists and KYC and AML norms when taking on new clients is of the essence for FIs to protect their operations and reputations.

Financial institutions are usually the ones who suffer the most risk and compliance issues from possibly sanctioned clients. Many sanctioned entities use discrete methods to shield their true identities. This helps them go undetected by sanction screening lists and watchlists. Many financial institutions and companies dealing with foreign entities have taken to using sanction screening lists to detect illicit actors. However, the entities in sanctioned jurisdictions use innovative ways to make sure that they are able to carry out their normal trading and financial activities despite the sanctions on them.

HOW OFTEN SHOULD SANCTIONS SCREENING TAKE PLACE?

Sanctions screening should be conducted on a regular basis to ensure that the bank is complying with applicable sanctions laws and regulations. The frequency of screening will depend on a number of factors, including the size of the bank, the complexity of its operations, the countries and regions in which it does business, and the level of risk associated with its customers and transactions.

In general, banks should conduct sanctions screening on a continuous or near-continuous basis, with real-time screening of transactions as they are processed. This can help to ensure that any potential violations are identified and addressed as quickly as possible.

In addition to real-time screening, banks should also conduct periodic screening of their customer base and other parties with which they do business. The frequency of this screening will depend on the level of risk associated with the customers and transactions, but it is generally recommended that screening be conducted at least once a year.

It's important to note that the frequency of sanctions screening should be reviewed regularly and adjusted as necessary to ensure that the bank is meeting its compliance obligations.

SANCTION SCREENING TECHNOLOGIES

Sanction screening technologies can help to improve the efficiency and effectiveness of sanctions compliance by automating the process of scanning large volumes of data. However, it is important for entities to ensure that the tools are used effectively and that compliance staff are trained to identify and resolve potential matches.

LIST-BASED SCREENING TOOLS

These tools are the most basic type of sanction screening technology. They work by comparing customer and transaction data against lists of sanctioned entities, countries, and individuals provided by government agencies such as the U.S. Office of Foreign Assets Control (OFAC). The lists can be either downloaded and updated manually or automatically by the screening tool. These tools are simple to use and relatively inexpensive, but they may generate a high number of false positives, which require further investigation by compliance staff.

RULES-BASED SCREENING TOOLS

These tools use a set of predefined rules to screen customer and transaction data for potential sanctions risks. For example, a rule may be set to flag any transaction with a high value going to a sanctioned country. The rules can be customized to fit an entity's specific risk profile and can be updated as needed. These tools are more sophisticated than list-based screening tools, but they still may generate a high number of false positives and require further investigation by compliance staff.

AI-BASED SCREENING TOOLS

These tools use machine learning algorithms to identify potential matches to sanctions lists and other regulatory requirements. They can be trained to recognize patterns and anomalies in transaction and customer data that may indicate potential sanctions risks. AI-based screening tools are more accurate than list-based and rules-based screening tools, but they require significant resources and expertise to develop and maintain.

AUTOMATED SCREENING TOOLS

Automated screening tools are software programs that use algorithms to screen large volumes of data for potential matches to predefined criteria or lists. In the context of sanctions compliance, automated screening tools are used to scan transactions, customers, and other data for potential matches to sanctions lists and other regulatory requirements.

For example, a bank may use automated screening tools to scan all incoming and outgoing wire transfers for potential matches to OFAC's sanctions lists. The software program would compare the information in the wire transfer to the information in the sanctions lists and flag any potential matches for further review by compliance staff.

Automated screening tools can help to improve the efficiency and effectiveness of sanctions screening by automating the process of scanning large volumes of data. This can help to reduce the risk of human error and enable compliance staff to focus on higher-risk transactions and customers.

However, it is important to note that automated screening tools are not foolproof and can generate false positives or miss potential matches. Therefore, it is important for entities to have effective procedures in place to review and resolve potential matches and to ensure that compliance staff are trained to use the tools effectively.

INTERDICTION SOFTWARE

Interdiction software, also known as sanctions screening software or sanctions compliance software, is a type of software designed to assist entities in complying with economic sanctions. Interdiction software works by screening names, addresses, and other information against a variety of sanctions lists and databases, and alerting users if a potential match is found.

Interdiction software can be used by financial institutions, businesses, and other organizations to ensure compliance with sanctions laws and regulations. By using interdiction software, entities can quickly and efficiently screen customers, counterparties, and other parties for potential sanctions risks, and take appropriate action if a match is found.

Credit Suisse allegedly facilitated transactions involving countries and entities subject to U.S. sanctions, including Iran, Sudan, and Syria. The bank was accused of using cover payments and other techniques to conceal the involvement of sanctioned entities in these transactions.

In addition to the sanctions violations, Credit Suisse was also accused of failing to implement effective sanctions compliance controls. As part of the settlement, Credit Suisse agreed to implement a series of remedial measures, including the improvement of its sanctions compliance program and the use of enhanced screening measures, such as interdiction software, to identify potential sanctions risks.

BLOCKCHAIN ANALYSIS TOOLS

These tools use blockchain technology to trace the flow of funds on the blockchain and identify potential sanctions risks. They can be used to monitor cryptocurrency transactions and identify any links to sanctioned entities or countries. Blockchain analysis tools are still in the early stages of development and are not yet widely available.

WOLFSBERG SCREENING GUIDANCE

The Wolfsberg Group is an association of thirteen global banks which aims to develop frameworks and guidance for the management of financial crime risks, including money laundering, terrorist financing, and sanctions compliance. The Wolfsberg Group has published several guidance documents, including the Wolfsberg Correspondent Banking Due Diligence Questionnaire, the Wolfsberg Anti-Money Laundering Principles for Private Banking, and the Wolfsberg Trade Finance Principles.[x]

One of the key guidance documents published by the Wolfsberg Group is the Wolfsberg Screening Guidance, which provides guidance on the design and implementation of screening processes to identify sanctioned parties. The guidance covers a range of topics, including the importance of having a clear screening policy, the use of appropriate data sources, the frequency of screening, the use of automated screening tools, and the need for effective governance and oversight of the screening process.

The Wolfsberg Screening Guidance is intended to help financial institutions meet their regulatory obligations related to sanctions compliance, and to ensure that their screening processes are effective in identifying sanctioned parties and mitigating the risk of sanctions breaches.

Wolfsberg Screening Guidance provides several key definitions related to screening. These definitions include:

FUZZY MATCHING

In the context of sanctions screening, "fuzzy matching" refers to the use of algorithms to identify potential matches between the names of individuals or entities being screened and the names on sanctions lists. Fuzzy matching algorithms are designed to account for variations in spellings, formats, and other differences in the names being compared, in order to identify potential matches that might be missed by an exact match search.

The Wolfsberg Screening Guidance, published by the Wolfsberg Group of international banks, provides recommendations and best practices for sanctions screening, including the use of fuzzy matching algorithms. The guidance suggests that banks should use a combination of exact and fuzzy matching algorithms, with different algorithms applied to different data fields and with different thresholds for triggering potential matches, depending on the level of risk associated with the transaction or relationship being screened.

Fuzzy matching is one of the several techniques used in sanctions screening to reduce the risk of false positives or false negatives, which can occur when an exact match search is used without taking into account variations in name spellings or formats.

NAME SCREENING

The Wolfsberg Screening Guidance recommends using an automated name matching system that includes fuzzy matching capabilities, which can help to identify potential matches even when the names on the sanctions list are misspelled, abbreviated, or translated into a different language.

The guidance also recommends using additional data fields, such as date of birth, nationality, and address, to help confirm or rule out potential matches. The screening system should also be regularly reviewed and updated to ensure that it is operating effectively and that it incorporates the latest sanctions lists and changes in customer information. Finally, the guidance emphasizes the importance of a risk-based approach to customer name matching, which involves prioritizing high-risk customers for closer scrutiny and applying appropriate levels of due diligence based on the level of risk.

In name screening, financial institutions simply run the client's name through a software programme, in order to detect sanctioned entities. Individual clients may be a part of larger, sanctioned organizations. they may also hold high-ranking positions in the governments of sanctioned countries.

Name screening can help to expose Politically Exposed Persons (PEPs) and people with criminal histories. It can help banks choose which customers to welcome onboard, without dealing with complications from non-disclosure of sanctions.

However, name-screening programs must be designed to carry out in-depth screening and provide fuzzy matches. Sanctioned individuals may provide slightly altered details so that screening programs do not pick up on their names.

These programs must be able to provide close matches so that such individuals do not go undetected. Sometimes, the Romanised translations of foreigners' names may vary. The system must keep track of this too.

NAME SCREENING TOOL

Though there are many commercial tools available for name search, one of the most important name screening tools is Sanctions List Search.

Sanctions List Search is a free tool provided by the U.S. Treasury Department's Office of Foreign Assets Control (OFAC). It allows users to search for individuals and entities on OFAC's list of Specially Designated Nationals and Blocked Persons (SDN List) and other sanctions lists

As an instance, when a bank or financial institution is presented with a payment or transfer request containing the name of an individual or entity that corresponds to an entry on a sanctions list, the bank's screening software will identify the name and the transaction for additional scrutiny. Compliance officers will then conduct a thorough examination to ascertain the validity of the match and make a decision regarding the approval or rejection of the transaction. If the name is a match, the bank must take appropriate action to comply with sanctions laws and regulations, which may include rejecting the transaction and reporting it to relevant authorities

Hence, the program must be efficient and updated in accordance to all sanction-implementing bodies.

TRANSACTION SCREENING

The Wolfsberg Screening Guidance provides guidance on transaction screening, which is the process of screening transactions against sanctions lists to identify potential matches. The guidance recommends that financial institutions implement a risk-based approach to transaction screening, taking into account factors such as the nature and complexity of the institution's operations, the risk profile of its customers, and the volume and frequency of its transactions.

The guidance recommends that financial institutions use a combination of automated and manual screening processes to identify potential matches. Automated screening involves using software to compare transaction data against sanctions lists, while manual screening involves a human reviewer reviewing transactions that have been flagged by the automated screening process.

The guidance emphasizes the importance of conducting ongoing monitoring of transactions, as well as periodic reviews of the institution's transaction screening processes to ensure that they remain effective and up to date with the latest regulatory and industry developments. Additionally, the guidance encourages financial institutions to document their transaction screening processes and to maintain appropriate records for audit and regulatory purposes.

SANCTION SCREENING LIST

Sanction lists are databases maintained by governments and international organizations that contain the names of individuals, organizations, and countries subject to sanctions. These lists are used to screen transactions and prevent financial institutions, businesses, and individuals from engaging in prohibited activities with sanctioned parties. Sanction lists typically include information such as the name, address, and identifying information of the sanctioned party, as well as the reason for the sanctions and the scope of the restrictions.

MAJOR SANCTION SCREENING LISTS

There are several major sanction screening databases used by financial institutions and other organizations for compliance purposes. These include:

- OFAC (Office of Foreign Assets Control) - The Office of Foreign Assets Control (OFAC) is a division of the U.S. Department of Treasury that administers and enforces economic and trade sanctions based on U.S. foreign policy and national security goals. OFAC maintains a list of Specially Designated Nationals and Blocked Persons (SDN List) which includes individuals and entities subject to sanctions and restrictions.

- EU Sanctions List[xi] - The European Union (EU) also maintains a consolidated list of sanctions targets, which is updated regularly. The list is maintained by the European External Action Service (EEAS) and includes individuals, organizations, and countries subject to EU sanctions.

- UN Sanctions List[xii] - The United Nations (UN) maintains a list of individuals and entities subject to sanctions, known as the Consolidated United Nations Security Council Sanctions List. This list includes individuals, groups, and entities involved in activities such as terrorism, nuclear proliferation, and other threats to international peace and security.

- UK[xiii]: The United Kingdom (UK) maintains its own list of sanctioned individuals and entities, which is updated regularly by the Office of Financial Sanctions Implementation (OFSI). The list includes both UK and non-UK individuals and entities, and may include individuals and entities that are not on other lists.

- DFAT Sanctions List[xiv] - The Australian Department of Foreign Affairs and Trade (DFAT) maintains a list of individuals and entities subject to sanctions, which is updated regularly. The list includes individuals, groups, and entities involved in activities such as terrorism, weapons proliferation, and other threats to international peace and security.

- SECO Sanctions List - This list is maintained by State Secretariat for Economic Affairs (SECO) and contains the names of individuals, organizations, and entities that are subject to financial sanctions imposed by Switzerland. The purpose of the SECO Sanctions List is to ensure compliance with international sanctions regimes and prevent the designated parties from accessing the Swiss financial system.

- JSE Sanctions List – JSE stands for "Japan's Specific Economic Measures". It refers to the set of specific economic sanctions imposed by the Japanese government on individuals, entities, or countries for various reasons such as national security concerns, international obligations, or policy objectives. The JSE sanctions are designed to restrict certain financial activities, trade transactions, or other economic interactions with the targeted individuals or entities. The JSE sanctions regime is maintained and enforced by the Japanese government to ensure compliance and adherence to the imposed restrictions.

- CAATSA[xv]: The Countering America's Adversaries Through Sanctions Act (CAATSA) is a U.S. law that imposes sanctions on individuals and entities in response to Russian aggression, human rights abuses, and other activities. The law includes a list of individuals and entities subject to sanctions, known as the CAATSA List.

- OSFI: The Canadian Office of the Superintendent of Financial Institutions (OSFI) is responsible for implementing financial sanctions in Canada. OSFI maintains a list of individuals and entities subject to financial sanctions, which is updated regularly.

- HKMA[xvi]: The Hong Kong Monetary Authority (HKMA) maintains a list of individuals and entities subject to sanctions in Hong Kong, which is updated regularly.

Many financial institutions, especially those dealing with international banks, maintain sanctions screening lists. These lists may contain information about politically exposed persons, terrorists and other suspicious people. In some cases, the FI may have to deal with a company which has a sanctioned or suspicious person on its board of directors. They may also unknowingly be dealing with a shell company formed by a sanctioned country. Many countries use innovative ways to bypass the Sanction Risk put on them and re-enter the international financial market.

To avoid falling into the trap of these entities, financial organizations screen their clients against a number of these lists. Collectively, these lists are called 'Sanctions Lists'. Screening can be a long and tedious process, and they need to apply thorough due diligence and weed out any dubious individuals.

Governing bodies like the Office of Foreign Assets Control (OFAC), The United Nations and the European Union maintain a database of all sanctioned entities. They share these lists with all high-ranking banks and other financial entities. Simply checking the details of the client's board of directors is not enough. The database and lists must include details of all associated customers, employees, suppliers and directors of the company.

WEAK ALIASES

Low quality aliases are names or terms that are vague, incomplete, or ambiguous, making it difficult to match them to an actual entity or individual. Examples of low-quality aliases include "John D" or "ABC Corp." without any additional identifying information. Other examples might include using initials or abbreviations that are not commonly recognized or using incomplete names, such as only providing a first name or a nickname. In general, low-quality aliases can increase the risk of false positives and require additional investigation to determine if a potential match is a true sanction hit.

The Wolfsberg Screening Guidance recommends that screening systems should have the ability to identify and manage low-quality aliases or nicknames to improve screening effectiveness. These are alternate names that do not meet the standard requirements for a full name match, but may still be used to refer to a sanctioned individual or entity.

To address this, the guidance recommends the use of advanced screening techniques, such as fuzzy matching, to identify possible matches between low-quality aliases and sanctioned entities or individuals. It also suggests that the screening system should be able to analyze and compare the context and frequency of use of these low-quality aliases in order to reduce false positives and improve the quality of matches.

POLITICALLY EXPOSED PERSONS

The definition of PEPs in the Wolfsberg Screening Guidance includes, but is not limited to, the following:

- Heads of state or government

- Senior politicians

- Senior government, judicial or military officials

- Senior executives of state-owned corporations

- Ambassadors and high-ranking diplomats

- High-ranking officials of international organizations

The term also includes the immediate family members and close associates of PEPs. PEPs are considered to pose a higher risk of corruption or bribery, and therefore, financial institutions are required to implement enhanced due diligence measures when dealing with them.

ALERT SPIKE

The term "alert spike" in Wolfsberg screening guidance refers to a sudden increase in the number of alerts generated by a sanctions screening system. This can occur due to various reasons, such as changes in the screening criteria, changes in the sanctions lists, changes in the customer base, or changes in the transaction patterns. An alert spike can indicate a potential breach of sanctions or other financial regulations and should be investigated promptly. It is important for banks and financial institutions to monitor alert spikes and take appropriate actions, such as reviewing the screening criteria, enhancing the customer due diligence process, and conducting deeper investigations into high-risk transactions or customers.

PROGRAMMATIC SANCTIONS RISK SCREENING

It may be very time-consuming for FIs to manually screen their clients against the sanctions lists. So, they have developed compliance software that helps detect and store all points of interest. These programs collect information about their clients and develop a risk-based score. The FI is then able to make decisions based on the results.

Programmatic Sanctions Screening takes many factors into account, only one of which is possible sanctions against the entity.

The sanctions detection programme in question must be up to date with all currently sanctioned entities, countries, and individuals. The programme must be in compliance with all the regulatory bodies' lists including the EU, OFAC, and the UN.

The programme must also be able to zone in on possible matches. It is not always granted that organizations will function under their true details once sanctioned. Many sanctioned entities make slight changes to their directors, organization names, and addresses to function under the radar. Hence, it is essential to fine-tune these programs enough for them to pick up on these slight changes and generate matches.

The programme must also be developed to store all data correctly and in an organized manner. All data collected by the programme during its searches must be easily accessible to its users. It must also be capable of generating reports on entities when and if needed. This helps in third-party functions like audits and inspections. This feature is known as audibility.

Practice Questions

What is the purpose of sanctions screening?

A) To help financial institutions identify high- risk customers and transactions

B) To prevent financial institutions from doing business with sanctioned entities

C) To provide financial institutions with an opportunity to earn more profits

D) To ensure compliance with international regulations and maintain global security

Answer: B

Which of the following is an example of a sanctions evasion technique?

A) Trade-based money laundering.

B) Know Your Customer (KYC) requirements.

C) Internal audit procedures.

D) Compliance training programs.

Answer: A

What is interdiction software?

A) Software used by authorities to monitor financial transactions

B) Software used by financial institutions to screen for sanctions

C) Software used by hackers to evade sanctions

D) Software used for analyzing financial transactions.

Answer: B

What is the Wolfsberg Screening Guidance?

A) A set of guidelines for conducting due diligence on customers

B) A set of guidelines for sanctions screening

C) A document outlining international trade policies.

D) A set of guidelines for anti-money laundering compliance

Answer: B

Which of the following is a key aspect of sanctions screening?

A) Ensuring maximum profits for financial institutions

C) Providing customers with the highest level of service

B) Maintaining accurate records of sanctions screening activities

D) Monitoring compliance with tax regulations.

Answer: B

What is the purpose of automated screening tools?

A) To provide a quick and efficient way of screening for sanctions

C) To increase the risk of false positives in sanctions screening

B) To replace human expertise in sanctions screening

D) To bypass regulatory requirements

Answer: A

SANCTIONS NON-COMPLIANCE

Sanctions are penalties regarding financial or commercial activities. A country or group of countries may put sanctions on another country, a group of people or organizations, or even an individual person. Though Sanctions themselves are essentially penalties, the consequences of breaking sanctions are even more severe.

The penalties for disobeying or disregarding sanctions depend on the body that puts the sanctions in place. The major bodies that have the authority to create and place sanctions are the OFAC, UN, EU and the OFSI.

Intergovernmental authorities consider sanctions as part of International Law, and it is illegal for any country, organization or individual to break sanctions placed on another entity.

CONSEQUENCES OF NON-COMPLIANCE

The consequences of non-compliance with sanctions depend on their nature.

In the United States, for example, non-compliance with sanctions is typically enforced by the Office of Foreign Assets Control (OFAC), a division of the U.S. Treasury Department. OFAC can impose both civil and criminal penalties for sanctions violations, including fines of up to millions of dollars and imprisonment of up to 30 years. OFAC can also freeze or block assets and transactions, and prohibit U.S. persons and entities from doing business with the violators.

It is expected that sanctioned entities only operate within their limits. If a sanctioned nation attempts to conduct trade outside of its jurisdiction, then it can suffer heavy penalties.

Most nations conduct trade with ships. Ships can help to transport large amounts of goods at a time and can access any nation's trading routes quite easily through their ports. Placing economic sanctions on countries essentially means putting a stop to their maritime trade activities. If any country or organization in the sanction watchlist attempts to move goods for export/import via sea, then the sanctioning body has the authority to seize and destroy the vessels in question.

Many sanctioned countries also unknowingly rope in ship providers and traders to transport their goods for them or illegally transport black money. This causes great harm to innocent parties if caught with the offending country's goods. Hence, International bodies advise that all companies that deal in maritime trade conduct extensive checks on the parties and clients they deal with on a regular basis.

If any multinational corporations, banks or other financial institutions break sanctions, then they may suffer unavoidable consequences. In many cases, the governing authority freezes their assets or levies heavy fines on them. Apart from this, they may also be branded as cooperative with criminals, which causes a heavy hit to their reputations.

NON-COMPLIANCE BY BUSINESS

One of the most high-profile cases in recent years was the sanctions violations committed by the Chinese tech giant ZTE Corporation. In 2017, ZTE was fined $1.19 billion by the US government for violating US sanctions on Iran and North Korea by selling technology to those countries. The US also banned American companies from doing business with ZTE for seven years, which threatened to put the company out of business. The ban was eventually lifted after ZTE agreed to pay an additional $1 billion fine and make changes to its management.

Another example is the Schlumberger Oilfield Holdings Ltd.

In 2015, the U.S. Treasury Department's Office of Foreign Assets Control (OFAC) announced a $232.7 million settlement with Schlumberger Oilfield Holdings Ltd., a subsidiary of Schlumberger Limited, for violating U.S. sanctions against Iran and Sudan. The company was found to have engaged in transactions with Iran and Sudan in violation of U.S. sanctions regulations.

NON-COMPLIANCE BY THE BANKS

In the history of the sanctions, banks have faced the major penalties for not complying with the sanctions.

- Société Générale S.A.: In 2018, French multinational bank Société Générale S.A. agreed to pay a $1.34 billion penalty for violating U.S. sanctions against Cuba, Iran, and Sudan. The bank was found to have processed thousands of transactions through U.S. financial institutions on behalf of clients in these sanctioned countries, in violation of U.S. sanctions regulations.

- Standard Chartered Bank: In 2019, Standard Chartered Bank agreed to pay a $1.1 billion penalty for violating U.S. sanctions against Iran. The bank was found to have processed millions of dollars in transactions on behalf of Iranian entities, in violation of U.S. sanctions regulations.

- BNP Paribas: In 2014, French bank BNP Paribas was fined $8.9 billion by the US government for violating US sanctions against Sudan, Cuba, and Iran. BNP Paribas was accused of processing transactions for these countries, which violated US sanctions laws.

- Commerzbank: In 2015, German bank Commerzbank was fined $1.45 billion by US regulators for violating US sanctions against Iran and Sudan. Commerzbank was accused of processing transactions for these countries, which violated US sanctions laws.

NON-COMPLIANCE BY INDIVIDUALS

The consequences for any individuals breaking sanction rules are rather similar to rules for entities and organizations. The most common consequences for individuals are implementing heavy fines on them or starting criminal proceedings. There are many examples of individuals violating sanctions. Here are a few notable examples:

1   Alexei Burkov: In 2019, Alexei Burkov, a Russian national, was arrested in Israel and later extradited to the United States for his alleged involvement in an

international cybercrime scheme. Burkov was accused of operating a website that facilitated the sale of stolen credit card information and other illegal goods. He was also accused of violating US sanctions by conducting business with individuals and companies in Iran.

2   Ali Sadr Hashemi Nejad: In 2018, Ali Sadr Hashemi Nejad, an Iranian national, was arrested in the United States for allegedly violating US sanctions by processing more than $115 million in payments for a Venezuelan construction project through US banks. Nejad was charged with conspiracy to commit bank fraud, money laundering, and violations of the International Emergency Economic Powers Act (IEEPA).

3   Dan Gertler: In 2017, Dan Gertler, an Israeli businessman and close associate of the former president of the Democratic Republic of the Congo, was sanctioned by the US Treasury Department for alleged human rights abuses and corrupt business practices in the Congo. Gertler was accused of using his close ties to the Congolese government to obtain valuable mining contracts and evade US sanctions.

According to the OFSI (Office of Financial Sanctions Implementation) of the UK, the penalty for serious financial breaches is set to around 1 million pounds or 50% of the amount lost during the breach- whichever is higher. The accused may also face up to seven years in jail.

The OFAC maintains two lists. The Specially Designed Nations lists contain records of international companies and individuals who have committed wrongdoings against the US. The other list, the Consolidated Sanctions Lists, contains a list of other parties that are on the Sanctions watchlist. The OFAC is generally stricter than the OFSI when it comes to penalties.

Anyone who breaks US/OFAC sanctions is subject to extremely heavy fines. This can range from a few thousand to millions of dollars, depending on the extent of the damage. Offenders also face prison time of up to 30 years.

IS ACCIDENTAL NON-COMPLIANCE PUNISHABLE?

Yes, non-compliance of all kinds- be it intentional or not- is subject to penalties. However, the extent of the punishment may vary on whether the bank performed the non-compliance intentionally or not. In cases where the non-compliant entity was unaware that it was dealing with sanctioned entities, it is still seen as negligence on their side. Banks and other organizations which operate on an international level must operate with KYC and AML regulations in mind.

Whenever a company breaks sanction rules, the OFAC or OFIS conducts a thorough analysis on whether it was intentional and the extent of the damage. Based on these two factors, it decides on how to penalize the offending entity. Organizations that have shown similar behaviour in the past are fined heavily for non-compliance and recurring negligence. In some cases, if the consequences are extremely severe, then they may also lose their business and assets.

INVESTIGATING SANCTIONS BREACH ALLEGATIONS

On completion of the certification programs one of the jobs that Certified Sanctions Expert do is to investigate the sanctions breaches for the banks. Investigating sanctions breach allegations can be a complex and challenging process, requiring a thorough understanding of the relevant laws and regulations, as well as the ability to gather and analyze a wide range of information.

Here are some general steps that can be taken when investigating allegations of sanctions breaches:

- Determine the scope of the investigation: This involves identifying the nature of the alleged breach, the individuals or entities involved, and the potential impact on the company and its stakeholders.

- Assemble an investigation team: This team should include individuals with relevant expertise in areas such as compliance, legal, and financial investigations. It is important to ensure that the team is independent and has the necessary resources to conduct a thorough investigation.

- Collect and review relevant information: This may include reviewing documents and communications, interviewing employees and third-party individuals or entities, and analyzing financial transactions.

- Conduct a risk assessment: Assess the potential impact of the alleged breach, including financial and reputational risks, and consider the potential legal and regulatory consequences.

- Determine the appropriate course of action: Depending on the findings of the investigation, the company may need to take corrective actions, such as implementing new compliance policies or terminating relationships with sanctioned entities. In some cases, self-disclosure and cooperation with regulators may be required.

- Communicate findings and take remedial action: If the investigation uncovers evidence of sanctions breaches, the company should communicate the findings to relevant stakeholders, including regulators and business partners. The company should also take steps to address the issues and prevent future breaches from occurring.

INVESTIGATING THE FINANCIAL INSTITUTIONS FOR BREACH

OFAC Investigated BNP Paribas for its violation of the regulations. Additionally, the European Union (EU) has investigated and imposed sanctions on various financial institutions and individuals for breaching sanctions. Some examples include:

- Swift (Society for Worldwide Interbank Financial Telecommunication): In 2012, the EU imposed sanctions on Swift, which is based in Belgium, for facilitating transactions involving Iranian banks that were under sanctions. The EU later lifted the sanctions after Swift agreed to stop processing transactions for the sanctioned Iranian banks.

- ING Bank: In 2012, the EU imposed sanctions on ING Bank, a Dutch bank, for violating sanctions against Iran and Cuba. The bank was fined €619 million for processing transactions that involved the sanctioned countries.

- Clearstream Banking: In 2008, the EU imposed sanctions on Clearstream Banking, a Luxembourg-based financial institution, for facilitating illegal arms sales to Angola. The sanctions were lifted in 2009 after the institution agreed to cooperate with the investigation.

Regulatory bodies may receive allegations related to financial institutions breaching sanctions from many sources. They may be from employees, anonymous tip hotlines, the press, or regulators. These allegations must be taken extremely seriously, as they can cause severe damage to the involved bank's reputation.

The steps for conducting a proper sanctions breach investigation are-

IDENTIFYING THE FI'S INTENTIONS

The investigator must first attempt to identify the purpose behind the transactions. In some cases, financial institutions may have knowingly and willfully violated sanctions, with the intention of profiting from prohibited transactions. In other cases, the breach of sanctions may have been the result of inadequate controls or lack of understanding of the regulations, rather than a deliberate attempt to evade sanctions. A person breaching sanctions is most likely involved in illicit activities. Tracing the source and destination of the transactions can help to determine the true purpose of the client's actions.

The team must also review whether the bank was an intentional party. Did they intentionally breach the sanctions in return for compensation, or were their actions due to negligence?

The investigators must also keep the geographical scope in question. They must check if the bank has in fact broken any laws of the country they are situated in, as each area has different stances on the same issue.

COLLECTING DOCUMENTATION

Next, they must collect all necessary documentation. They must collect data on each and every transaction that took place during the reported time period.

The first step is to identify the types of documents that are relevant to the investigation. This could include transaction records, account opening documents, communication logs, and compliance policies and procedures.

They must also collect emails, letters, and other means of correspondence. The investigators will run these documents through sanctions screening programs to detect keywords and create an audit trail.

After the documents have been obtained, they should be reviewed to identify potential violations of sanctions regulations. This could involve comparing the transaction data against a sanctions list, analyzing the purpose and nature of the transaction, or reviewing communications for evidence of sanctions evasion. relevant documents should be maintained for a certain period of time to ensure that they can be easily accessed if needed for future investigations or audits. The specific retention requirements may vary depending on the type of document and applicable regulations.

INTERVIEWING WITNESSES AND COLLECTING INFORMATION

The team may also decide to interview key witnesses and employees. This includes the whistleblower on the situation. Interviewing people can help gain different accounts and points of view on the same situation. If there is an intentional sanction evasion then the trails of the same would not be available through the transaction papers unless some one speaks that in an interview.

Interviews provide an opportunity to gather information from individuals who may have knowledge of the breach or related transactions. This information can be used to build a more complete picture of the breach and to identify other individuals who may be involved. They may also uncover crucial evidence through these interviews, which they can then follow up on. Interviews can help investigators to assess the credibility of the information provided by individuals.

This can be done by asking follow-up questions, verifying information provided, and comparing information from multiple sources. Interviews can be used to obtain admissions from individuals involved in the breach. This can be done by asking direct questions about the individual's involvement and using the information obtained during the interview to build a case against them.

PREPARING REPORTS

Once they finish the initial investigation, the team must prepare a report on their findings. The report must include their methods of investigation, which measures they use to detect sanction breaches and all the evidence that led them to their final decision. They must also note down all the assets and funds involved in the case. If a watch-listed entity breaches sanctions, then the governing body will freeze or seize its assets. Hence, the investigators must include a comprehensive list of all assets involved.

Finally, they must advise the bank or financial institution on how to proceed with their operations so that this doesn't happen again. if the bank is a willing conspirator, then the OFAC or OFSI is notified, and they deal with their institution. In the case that the bank did not co-operate with the clients knowingly, they will draft preventive measures to abide by in the future. If the company follows these rules, then they do not need to be formally apprehended.

Practice Questions

What is the first step in collecting documentation during a sanctions breach investigation?

A) Preserving the documents

B) Obtaining the documents

C) Reviewing the documents

D) Identifying the relevant documents

Answer: D

Why is interviewing important in sanctions investigations?

A) To establish intent

B) To preserve evidence

C) To review policies and procedures

D) To analyze transaction data

Answer: A

What is the purpose of reviewing collected documents during a sanctions investigation?

A) To identify potential violations of sanctions regulations

B) To request additional documents from employees

C) To preserve evidence

D) To review policies and procedures

Answer: A

What should be included in a report documenting the findings of a sanctions breach investigation?

A) The suspected breach, evidence gathered, and analysis conducted

B) The names and contact information of individuals interviewed

C) The specific retention requirements for each document reviewed

D) A summary of the institution's compliance policies and procedures

Answer: A.

ROLE OF FINANCIAL ACTION TASK FORCE

The G7 countries created the FATF, an intergovernmental body, in 1989. The purpose of the FATF is to keep a close eye on any cross-border money laundering activities taking place. While FATF's primary focus is not on sanctions, it has played a role in supporting international sanctions regimes.

FINANCIAL ACTION TASK FORCE

The FATF has developed a series of Recommendations that are recognised as the international standard for combating of money laundering and the financing of terrorism and proliferation of weapons of mass destruction. They form the basis for a co-ordinated response to these threats to the integrity of the financial system and help ensure a level playing field. FATF's work on proliferation financing, which refers to the financing of weapons of mass destruction and their means of delivery, is closely linked to sanctions. Proliferation financing can be used to circumvent sanctions, and FATF has developed guidance to help countries implement measures to detect and prevent such activities.

FATF also maintains a list of countries that have strategic deficiencies in their anti-money laundering and counter-terrorist financing (AML/CFT) regimes.

Additionally, FATF contributes to sanctions enforcement by conducting assessments of countries' anti-money laundering and counter-terrorist financing (AML/CFT) regimes. As part of these assessments, FATF evaluates whether countries have implemented measures to comply with UN sanctions and other international sanctions regimes, and whether they are effectively enforcing them.

The Financial Action Task Force (FATF) has developed a set of 40 recommendations that provide a comprehensive framework for countries to combat money laundering, terrorist financing, and other threats to the integrity of the international financial system. These recommendations serve as international standards and are widely recognized and implemented by countries around the world.

Each recommendation plays a vital role in establishing a comprehensive and robust anti-money laundering and counter-terrorist financing regime. The effective implementation of all recommendations is crucial to combat financial crimes and protect the integrity of the global financial system. While recommendations 6 and 7 specifically target areas related to sanctions and their enforcement, the other 38 recommendations of the FATF cover various aspects of anti-money laundering and counter-terrorist financing, including risk assessments, customer due diligence, reporting suspicious transactions, international cooperation, and legal frameworks.

FATF RECOMMENDATION 6

FATF Recommendation 6 is one of the 40 recommendations developed by the Financial Action Task Force (FATF) to combat money laundering, terrorist financing, and other threats to the integrity of the global financial system.

This recommendation specifically deals with the use of targeted financial sanctions related to terrorism and terrorist financing.

Under Recommendation 6, countries are required to implement targeted financial sanctions against individuals and entities designated as terrorists or terrorist organizations. These sanctions may include freezing of assets, blocking of transactions, and prohibiting access to financial services. The purpose of these targeted financial sanctions is to disrupt the financial networks of terrorists and their supporters, and to prevent them from accessing the resources which they need for carrying out their activities.

In addition, countries are required to implement measures to prevent the provision of financial services to individuals and entities designated as terrorists or terrorist organizations. Financial institutions are required to conduct enhanced due diligence on customers, monitor transactions for suspicious activity, and report any suspicious transactions to the appropriate authorities.

The FATF monitors compliance with Recommendation 6 through its mutual evaluation process, which assesses the effectiveness of a country's anti-money laundering and counter-terrorist financing regime. Countries that do not comply with the recommendations may be subject to a range of measures, including public statements, sanctions, and restrictions on financial flows.

FATF RECOMMENDATION 7

FATF Recommendation 7 is one of the 40 recommendations developed by the Financial Action Task Force (FATF) to combat money laundering, terrorist financing, and the proliferation of weapons of mass destruction. This recommendation specifically deals with the use of targeted financial sanctions related to proliferation.

Under Recommendation 7, countries are required to implement targeted financial sanctions against individuals and entities involved in the proliferation of weapons of mass destruction, including nuclear, chemical, and biological weapons. These sanctions may include freezing of assets, blocking of transactions, and prohibiting access to financial services. The purpose of these targeted financial sanctions is to prevent the financing of proliferation activities and to disrupt the financial networks of proliferators.

In addition, countries are required to implement measures to prevent the provision of financial services to individuals and entities involved in proliferation activities. Financial institutions are required to conduct enhanced due diligence on customers, monitor transactions for suspicious activity, and report any suspicious transactions to the appropriate authorities.

The FATF monitors compliance with Recommendation 7 through its mutual evaluation process, which assesses the effectiveness of a country's anti-money laundering and counter-terrorist financing regime. Countries that do not comply with the recommendations may be subject to a range of measures, including public statements, sanctions, and restrictions on financial flows

GUIDANCE ON PROLIFERATION FINANCE

The FATF guidance on proliferation financing is closely related to sanctions as it provides guidelines to countries and financial institutions on how to prevent the financing of activities related to the proliferation of weapons of mass destruction (WMDs). The proliferation of WMDs is a serious global security threat, and many countries have implemented sanctions regimes to prevent it.

Sanctions can be used to target individuals, entities, and countries involved in the proliferation of WMDs by imposing restrictions on their ability to access financial services and trade. The FATF guidance on proliferation financing helps to ensure that financial institutions are equipped with the necessary tools and knowledge to prevent the financing of WMD proliferation activities and to comply with relevant sanctions.

The Proliferation Financing Guidance Note, or PFGN, is a document developed by the Financial Action Task Force (FATF) that provides guidance to countries and the private sector on how to identify, assess, and respond to proliferation financing risks.

Proliferation financing refers to the financing of the proliferation of weapons of mass destruction (WMD) and their delivery systems. This can include the financing of nuclear, chemical, and biological weapons, as well as ballistic missiles and other delivery systems.

The PFGN is designed to help countries and the private sector understand the nature of proliferation financing risks and to provide guidance on how to develop effective risk-based approaches to preventing and detecting proliferation financing. The guidance includes:

- Understanding proliferation financing risks: The PFGN provides guidance on how to assess the risks associated with proliferation financing, including the types of actors and activities involved in proliferation financing, and the methods and techniques used to move and conceal funds.

- Developing risk-based approaches: The PFGN provides guidance on how to develop effective risk-based approaches to identifying and addressing proliferation financing risks. This includes guidance on how to implement appropriate customer due diligence measures, transaction monitoring, and other measures to detect and prevent proliferation financing.

- Sharing information: The PFGN emphasizes the importance of information sharing among countries and between the public and private sectors in detecting and preventing proliferation financing. The guidance provides recommendations on how to share information effectively and securely while protecting confidentiality and data privacy.

- Responding to proliferation financing: The PFGN provides guidance on how to respond to proliferation financing, including how to freeze and seize assets, impose sanctions, and take other measures to disrupt proliferation financing networks.

By following the FATF guidance, financial institutions can identify and report suspicious transactions related to the proliferation of WMDs.

FRAMEWORK UNDER PROLIFERATION FINANCE

In June 2021, the Financial Action Task Force (FATF) released updated guidance on countering the financing of proliferation (CFP), which refers to the provision of funds or financial services to individuals, entities, or governments involved in the development, acquisition, production, or use of weapons of mass destruction (WMD) or their delivery systems.

The new guidance provides a comprehensive framework for identifying, assessing, and mitigating the risks associated with CFP. The key elements of the guidance include:

1   National risk assessment: Countries are encouraged to conduct a comprehensive risk assessment of CFP and develop a national strategy to address the identified risks.

2   Understanding the risk: Financial institutions are expected to identify, assess, and understand the risks associated with CFP, including the types of proliferation financing methods, typologies, and trends.

3   Customer due diligence (CDD): Financial institutions are required to perform enhanced due diligence (EDD) when dealing with higher-risk customers and transactions, including those involving jurisdictions and individuals/entities associated with proliferation financing.

4   Monitoring and reporting: Financial institutions are expected to have effective systems in place to monitor and report suspicious transactions related to CFP.

5   Cooperation and information-sharing: Countries and financial institutions are encouraged to cooperate and share information domestically and internationally to enhance the effectiveness of CFP measures.

6   Sanctions and other measures: Countries are expected to implement targeted financial sanctions and other measures against individuals and entities involved in

CFP, and financial institutions are required to freeze and report assets of designated persons and entities.

FATF LISTS

The FATF currently has two lists- the grey list and the Black list- which it uses to classify countries of concern. It maintains a list of countries that it has identified as having strategic deficiencies in their anti-money laundering and counter-terrorist financing (AML/CFT) regimes. This list is commonly known as the "FATF Blacklist" or "FATF Non-Compliant List."

These countries are subject to enhanced due diligence measures by financial institutions to prevent money laundering and terrorist financing. FATF encourages its members to consider implementing countermeasures against these countries, which may include measures such as increased scrutiny of transactions, restrictions on correspondent banking relationships, and limiting access to the international financial system.

Countries on the Grey List do not suffer as severe repercussions as those on the Black List. The FATF places countries that turn a blind eye toward the spread of blatant money laundering and terror funding on the Black List. The FATF has likely observed the beginnings of such activities in Grey-Listed countries. Placing a country on the Grey List serves as a sort of warning for them. If they do not take any action against the spread of such activities, the FATF will most likely move them to the Black List.

WHAT HAPPENS TO A GREY-LISTED COUNTRY?

Though being on the Grey List does not seem as severe as being on the Black List, these countries may still face some repercussions. When a country is placed on the grey list, it comes with the stigma of being an unreliable trade partner. Many countries may reduce their trading channels to and from the affected country. They may also stop imports and exports to and from the Grey-listed country entirely. This can severely affect the country's economy and international trade.

International bodies like the IMF and World Bank may also put financial and economic sanctions on the Grey-listed country. They may refuse to provide them with any loans until they start making serious efforts to combat these issues. The FATF may even blacklist the country if the government is not able to suppress the financial crimes taking place.

If a country doesn't cooperate with the FATF, it blacklists them. They may either legally be unequipped, or unwilling to provide foreign law officials with any information regarding the current matters in their country. A country must also be willing to cooperate with all other member countries to help combat cross-border money laundering.

Placing a country on the grey list is essentially placing financial sanctions on it. If the country neglects to follow the sanctions, then the FATF places them on the black list. When the FATF puts a country on the black list, it suffers the same economic impact as OFAC and OFSI sanctions.

Practice Questions

What is the purpose of the FATF's Proliferation Finance Guidance?

A) To combat money laundering

B) To combat terror financing

C) To combat the financing of the proliferation of weapons of mass destruction (WMD)

D) To combat tax evasion

Answer: C

What is the primary objective of the FATF when it comes to proliferation financing?

A) To prevent the transfer of WMDs

B) To prevent the financing of WMD proliferation

C) To track the source of WMDs

D) To prevent the use of WMDs in terrorist activities

Answer: B

What entities are primarily targeted under the FATF's Proliferation Finance Guidance?

A) Governments and state-owned enterprises

B) Charities and non-governmental organizations (NGOs)

C) Financial institutions and their customers

D) Corporations engaged in international trade

Answer: C

What are some of the red flags that could indicate potential proliferation financing?

A) Transactions with countries subject to sanctions

B) Unusual payment patterns or payment methods

C) Shipping goods to high-risk jurisdictions

D) All of the above

Answer: D

SANCTIONS COMPLIANCE PROGRAM

A sanctions compliance program is a set of measures that a company puts in place to ensure that it does not violate sanctions regulations.

SANCTIONS COMPLIANCE PROGRAM

A comprehensive sanctions compliance program is a set of policies, procedures, and controls put in place by a company or organization to ensure compliance with sanctions laws and regulations. The program is designed to identify, assess, and mitigate sanctions-related risks and to prevent the company from engaging in prohibited transactions. Some key elements of a comprehensive sanction's compliance program include:

- Risk assessment: The company should conduct an assessment of its business activities and assess the risk of exposure to sanctions violations.

- Policies and procedures: The company should develop and implement policies and procedures that reflect the risk assessment and provide guidance to employees on how to comply with sanctions regulations.

- Training: The company should provide regular training to employees on sanctions regulations and the company's policies and procedures.

- Internal controls: The company should implement internal controls to monitor and verify compliance with sanctions regulations and the company's policies and procedures.

- Due diligence: The company should conduct due diligence on its customers, suppliers, and other business partners to ensure that they are not involved in sanctions violations.

- Recordkeeping: The company should maintain accurate records of its compliance activities, including due diligence, training, and internal controls.

- Auditing and monitoring: The company should regularly audit and monitor its compliance program to ensure that it is effective and to identify and address any compliance gaps.

- Response and corrective action: The company should have a plan in place to respond to potential violations and to take appropriate corrective action if any violations occur.

Overall, a comprehensive sanctions compliance program should be tailored to the specific risks and needs of the company and should be regularly reviewed and updated to ensure its effectiveness.

SANCTIONS COMPLIANCE OFFICER

A sanctions compliance officer (SCO) is responsible for overseeing and implementing a company's sanctions compliance program. The SCO's role is to ensure that the company complies with relevant sanctions regulations and policies, and to establish procedures and controls to detect and prevent violations.

The specific responsibilities of an SCO may include:

- Developing and implementing sanctions policies and procedures.
- Providing guidance and training to employees and other stakeholders on sanctions compliance.
- Conducting risk assessments to identify areas of potential exposure to sanctions risks.
- Screening transactions, customers, suppliers, and other parties against sanctions lists.

- Investigating and resolving potential sanctions violations, and reporting any violations to relevant authorities.

- Keeping up-to-date with changes in sanctions regulations and guidelines, and ensuring that the company's compliance program remains current and effective.

- Collaborating with other departments and stakeholders within the company to ensure that the sanctions compliance program is integrated with other compliance initiatives.

Role of an SCO is critical in ensuring that a company's sanctions compliance program is effective and efficient in mitigating the risk of non-compliance. The SCO plays a key role in safeguarding the company's reputation and financial interests, and in maintaining the trust and confidence of stakeholders and regulators.

TESTING AND AUDITING

A robust system of internal controls is essential for a bank to maintain its security, safeguard its funds, and uphold its integrity. When a bank's internal controls are weak, it can cause negligence on its part when checking for sanctioned or blacklisted entities.

Auditing is an important step in ensuring that all the internal controls are up-to-date. Conducting timely audits can help to make sure that banks are dealing with their clients properly, and following the necessary guidelines.

WHAT IS TESTING?

Testing in terms of sanctions compliance refers to the process of evaluating and assessing the effectiveness of a financial institution's sanctions compliance program. The purpose of testing is to identify any weaknesses or gaps in the program and to provide recommendations for improvement. Testing can be conducted through various methods such as sample testing, transaction testing, scenario testing, and independent testing. It is an important part of a comprehensive sanctions compliance program as it helps to ensure that the institution is effectively managing sanctions risks and complying with applicable laws and regulations.

SAMPLE TESTING

Sample testing in the context of sanctions compliance program refers to the practice of selecting a representative sample of transactions, customers, or other relevant data and subjecting them to testing or analysis to assess the effectiveness of the sanctions screening process. The purpose of sample testing is to identify any gaps or weaknesses in the screening process, such as false negatives (missed matches) or false positives (false alarms), and to determine whether the screening process is operating in accordance with the bank's policies and procedures, regulatory requirements, and best practices.

Sample testing can involve both manual and automated testing, and can be performed on an ongoing basis or as part of periodic reviews. The results of sample testing are used to identify areas for improvement in the sanctions screening process, and to implement corrective actions to address any identified deficiencies. This helps to ensure that the bank is effectively mitigating the risk of sanctions violations and complying with applicable regulations

TRANSACTION TESTING

Transaction testing is a process of testing individual transactions for compliance with sanctions regulations. This involves selecting a sample of transactions and reviewing them to ensure that they comply with the bank's sanctions policies and procedures. The aim of transaction testing is to identify any potential weaknesses or gaps in the bank's sanctions compliance program, and to ensure that all transactions are screened and monitored in accordance with applicable sanctions regulations. Transaction testing can be conducted manually or with the use of automated transaction monitoring systems. It is an important component of a bank's overall sanctions compliance program and helps to ensure that the bank is effectively managing its sanctions risks.

SCENARIO TESTING

Scenario testing in sanctions compliance involves assessing the effectiveness of a financial institution's sanctions compliance program by testing its response to simulated scenarios that replicate potential sanctions risks. It involves the creation of hypothetical scenarios based on real-world events that could result in a sanctions violation, such as a customer attempting to transact with a sanctioned entity or a transaction that appears to be suspicious. The financial institution's response to the scenario is then evaluated to identify any weaknesses in its sanctions compliance program and to make necessary improvements to prevent future violations. Scenario testing is a proactive approach to identify potential risks and improve the sanctions compliance program's effectiveness.

INDEPENDENT TESTING

Independent testing of sanctions compliance refers to the process of evaluating and assessing the effectiveness of a financial institution's sanctions compliance program by an independent third party. This is done to ensure that the institution is effectively identifying, monitoring, and reporting potential sanctions risks, and that its policies and procedures are in compliance with regulatory requirements and industry best practices.

Independent testing typically involves a review of the institution's internal controls, risk assessment methodology, policies and procedures, employee training programs, and the effectiveness of its sanctions screening systems. The independent testing may be conducted by internal auditors or external consultants, depending on the size and complexity of the institution.

The results of independent testing are used to identify gaps or weaknesses in the institution's sanctions compliance program, which can be addressed through remedial actions or enhancements to the program. The testing also helps to demonstrate to regulators and other stakeholders that the institution is committed to maintaining a robust and effective sanctions compliance program.

WHAT IS AUDITING?

In the context of sanctions compliance, auditing refers to a systematic and independent examination of a bank's sanctions compliance program to assess whether it is operating effectively and efficiently in accordance with regulatory requirements and internal policies and procedures. The audit is typically conducted by an independent internal or external auditor who reviews all aspects of the sanctions compliance program, including the bank's policies and procedures, risk assessments, training, screening processes, testing, and monitoring.

The purpose of auditing is to identify any weaknesses or deficiencies in the sanctions compliance program and to provide recommendations for improvement. Auditing is an important component of a bank's overall sanctions compliance program and helps to ensure that the bank is effectively managing its sanctions risks.

PROCEDURE TO CONDUCT AUDIT

The procedure to audit sanctions compliance typically involves the following steps:

- Planning: The auditor should plan the audit in advance, which includes reviewing the applicable laws, regulations, and policies related to sanctions compliance.

- Gathering information: The auditor should gather information related to the organization's sanctions compliance program, such as policies and procedures, risk assessments, training materials, and testing results.

- Assessing the design and implementation of the program: The auditor should evaluate the design and implementation of the sanctions compliance program to determine whether it is appropriate and effective.

- Analyzing results: The auditor should analyze the results of the testing procedures to identify any weaknesses or deficiencies in the sanctions compliance program.
- Reporting: The auditor should prepare a report that summarizes the findings of the audit and provides recommendations for improving the organization's sanctions compliance program.
- Follow-up: The auditor should follow up on the recommendations made in the audit report to ensure that the organization has taken appropriate corrective actions.

HOW DOES AUDITING DIFFERS FROM TESTING?

Auditing and testing are both important components of a comprehensive sanctions' compliance program, but they serve different purposes.

Testing is the process of examining a sample of transactions or customer accounts to assess whether the sanctions screening process is working effectively. The focus of testing is to identify specific issues and areas of weakness in the program, and to provide recommendations for improvement.

Auditing, on the other hand, is a broader and more comprehensive review of the entire sanctions compliance program. It involves an independent assessment of the design and effectiveness of the program, including policies, procedures, controls, and training. The aim of auditing is to ensure that the program as a whole is working effectively to manage sanctions risks, and to provide assurance to senior management and regulators that the bank is in compliance with relevant laws and regulations.

While testing is a critical component of monitoring the ongoing effectiveness of the sanctions compliance program, auditing provides a higher-level review of the program and can help to identify gaps or weaknesses that may not be identified through testing alone. Both testing and auditing are important to maintain an effective sanctions compliance program.

COMMUNICATION AND TRAINING

The chain of command in an organization is extremely important. Each employee must know the proper procedures when dealing with a suspicious client.

Effective communication is necessary for sanctions compliance because it helps ensure that all relevant stakeholders within an organization are aware of and understand the sanctions requirements and the organization's compliance policies and procedures. This includes communication between different departments within the organization, as well as with external stakeholders such as customers, vendors, and regulatory bodies.

By effectively communicating sanctions compliance policies and procedures to all relevant stakeholders, organizations can ensure that everyone understands their roles and responsibilities, and is aware of the potential risks and consequences of noncompliance. Communication can also help to identify potential compliance gaps or issues, and allow for timely corrective action to be taken.

Additionally, effective communication can help to promote a culture of compliance within the organization, where all employees understand the importance of sanctions compliance and are committed to follow the established policies and procedures.

The level of information shared with each employee depends on their position and security level. However, even lower-ranking employees must know who to approach if they come across these situations.

Companies must hold training sessions for their employees on a regular basis. This will help them identify the risks that come with blacklisted and sanctioned clients. They must also give their employees the proper resources to report and deal with any cases they come across. The training must be updated on a periodic basis, as sanctions and evasion techniques are constantly changing.

KNOW YOUR CUSTOMER AND SANCTIONS

Sanction screenings are essentially a part of Anti-Money Laundering measures. This means that they have close ties with KYC (Know Your Customer) norms. KYC norms dictate that every customer must provide details about their financial and criminal background (if any) as well as details like their birthdate, address, etc.

KYC helps financial institutions to identify and manage sanctions risks by screening customers and their transactions against sanctions lists and conducting enhanced due diligence for high-risk customers. This is essential in helping FIs detect any politically associated individuals and former financial criminals, to protect their assets and reputation. Unknowingly dealing with such individuals may not only land them into trouble with the authorities but also prove dangerous to them in case they repeat their previous actions and default again.

KYC norms help to identify Politically Exposed Persons (PEPs), individuals dealing with sanctioned governments or organizations and fraudsters and defaulters. It is up to the banks to make sure that they have a database with all of their client's KYC information on hand.

Many PEPs and criminals usually rope in their close friends or family members to conduct their business dealings for them, in order to bypass sanctions screenings and function as normal. Hence, it is important for FIs to conduct thorough research on all of their associate and note them in the database.

Not complying with KYC measures themselves may also land FIs in hot water. In many countries, it is compulsory for banks and other financial institutions to comply with KYC norms. Not acting in accordance with sanction watchlists or dealing with sanctioned entities under the table can not only attract steep fines but also result in the freezing of the FI's assets. In extreme cases, authorities may shut down the banking corporation entirely.

FATF GUIDELINES ON KYC

The Financial Action Task Force (FATF) is an intergovernmental organization that sets global standards for anti-money laundering and countering the financing of terrorism (AML/CFT). While FATF does not directly deal with sanctions, its KYC guidelines can help financial institutions comply with sanctions requirements.

Under the FATF's Recommendation 10, financial institutions are required to implement a risk-based approach to customer due diligence (CDD), which includes obtaining information on the purpose and intended nature of the business relationship. This includes identifying the beneficial owner of the customer, who may be a politically exposed person (PEP) or a high-risk customer. FATF's guidance also emphasizes the importance of ongoing monitoring of customer accounts and transactions, as well as conducting periodic reviews to ensure that customer information is up-to-date and accurate.

Financial institutions are also encouraged to use technology and data analytics to enhance their KYC and transaction monitoring systems, and to share information with other financial institutions and government authorities as necessary. FATF's KYC guidelines provide a comprehensive framework for financial institutions to identify and manage the risks associated with money laundering, terror financing, and other financial crimes, which includes compliance with sanctions requirements.

Financial institutions should have policies and procedures in place for KYC and customer identification, including the collection of accurate and up-to-date customer identification data, such as name, address, date of birth, and other relevant information. They should also have systems in place to verify the identity of their customers, such as verifying their identity documents or using electronic identity verification tools.

KYC REQUIREMENTS FOR SHIPPING INDUSTRY

OFAC provides guidance to the shipping industry to help them better understand the sanctions regulations and how to comply with them. It also conducts industry outreach to promote awareness of sanctions requirements and to encourage industry best practices.

ROLE OF OFAC GUIDELINES FOR KYC

As a standard practice, those involved in the maritime petroleum shipping community, including vessel owners and operators, are advised to conduct KYC. OFAC identifies high-risk entities in the shipping industry, including those involved in the transport of sanctioned goods or those that have engaged in sanctions evasion.

- OFAC may add these entities, vessels and individuals to its Specially Designated Nationals and Blocked Persons (SDN) List, which prohibits US persons from doing business with them.

- OFAC has also published several guidance documents for the maritime industry to help them understand and comply with U.S. sanctions laws and regulations. These documents provide guidance on topics such as compliance programs, risk assessments, and sanctions screening

- In June 2020, OFAC implemented the "50% rule," which requires entities which are owned 50% or more by one or more sanctioned individuals or entities to be subject to the same sanctions as the sanctioned individuals or entities. This rule aims to prevent sanctioned individuals and entities from using front companies to circumvent sanctions. The 50% rule is commonly used in the context of sanctions programs targeting countries such as Iran, North Korea, and Russia. Under the rule, companies conducting business with entities in these countries must ensure that their business partners do not have any ownership ties to sanctioned individuals or entities, including through the 50% rule. Failure to comply with the 50% rule can result in penalties and legal action by OFAC.

KNOW YOUR VESSEL

KYC (Know Your Customer) is an important aspect of sanctions compliance, and it can also be applied to identify potential risks related to AIS (Automatic Identification System) manipulation in the shipping industry. AIS is a tracking system used to monitor the location and movement of ships, and it can be manipulated by vessels to conceal their true location or activities, which can be a potential risk for sanctions compliance.[xvii]

To mitigate these risks, KYC procedures should be implemented to verify the identity and activities of vessels and their owners/operators. This may involve obtaining information on vessel ownership, management, and control structures, as well as conducting due diligence on associated parties and their activities.

Some specific KYC measures that can be applied to address AIS manipulation risks include:

- Verifying vessel ownership and control: KYC procedures can be used to verify the identity of vessel owners and operators, as well as the extent of their control over the vessel. This can help to identify cases where a vessel may be under the control of an individual or entity subject to sanctions.

- Monitoring vessel movements: KYC procedures can be used to monitor vessel movements and identify any suspicious activities or anomalies in AIS data. This can help to identify cases where a vessel may be attempting to conceal its true location or activities.

- Conducting due diligence on associated parties: KYC procedures can be used to conduct due diligence on associated parties, such as charterers, brokers, and cargo owners. This can help to identify cases where these parties may be involved in illicit activities or have connections to sanctioned individuals or entities.

- Establishing risk-based procedures: KYC procedures should be established based on a risk-based approach that takes into account the specific risks associated with AIS manipulation and the shipping industry more broadly. This may involve setting up procedures to conduct additional due diligence on high-risk vessels or associated parties.

RESEARCH ON IMO NUMBERS

The International Maritime Organization (IMO) number is a unique identifier for ships, and it can be used to check sanctions compliance. Here are the steps to conduct research on IMO numbers:

- Obtain the IMO number: You can obtain the IMO number from the vessel's documentation, such as the bill of lading, or by searching for the vessel name on publicly available databases, such as Equasis[xviii] or MarineTraffic.

- Check the sanctions lists: Once you have the IMO number, you can check it against the various sanctions lists, such as the OFAC Specially Designated Nationals (SDN) list or the EU Consolidated List of Sanctions. If the vessel or its owner is on any of the sanctions lists, it may be subject to sanctions or restrictions.

- Check vessel ownership: You can also use the IMO number to check the ownership of the vessel. If the vessel is owned by a sanctioned entity, it may be subject to sanctions or restrictions.

- Check vessel history: You can use the IMO number to check the vessel's history, including its previous ports of call and any incidents or detentions. This can provide additional information on potential sanctions risks associated with the vessel.

- Conduct ongoing monitoring: It's important to conduct ongoing monitoring of the vessel and its associated parties, as sanctions lists and regulations can change frequently. Automated screening software can be used to continuously monitor the IMO number and associated parties for any changes or updates to the sanctions lists.

- It's important to note that conducting research on IMO numbers for sanctions compliance purposes can be complex and time-consuming, and it's recommended to seek the assistance of compliance professionals or specialized software solutions.

RESEARCH ON AIS MANIPULATIONS

AIS (Automatic Identification System) manipulation is a significant concern for sanctions compliance in the shipping industry. The following steps can be taken to conduct research on AIS manipulation to check sanctions compliance:

- Conduct a risk assessment: Before starting the research, it is important to conduct a risk assessment to determine the level of risk associated with AIS manipulation for the specific transaction or shipping route.

- Identify the vessel and shipping route: Once the level of risk has been determined, identify the vessel and shipping route for which the research needs to be conducted.

- Check AIS data: Check the AIS data for the identified vessel and shipping route. AIS data is publicly available and can be accessed through various online platforms. Analyze the data for any discrepancies or inconsistencies.

- Check vessel ownership: Check the ownership of the vessel and its registered country. If the vessel is owned by a sanctioned entity or registered in a sanctioned country, it may be an indication of potential sanctions violations.

- Conduct background checks: Conduct background checks on the vessel, its owners, and the shipping company. This can help identify any past sanctions violations or other red flags.

- Use specialized tools: There are specialized tools available that can help identify AIS manipulation. These tools use advanced algorithms to analyze the AIS data and detect any anomalies or suspicious activities.

- Document the findings: Document all the findings and analysis in a clear and concise manner. This can help support any potential sanctions compliance investigations or audits.

It is important to note that conducting research on AIS manipulation can be complex and requires specialized knowledge and expertise. It may be beneficial to consult with experts in the field or seek the assistance of specialized service providers.

POLICIES AND PROCEDURES

An effective sanctions compliance program will require at least the following procedures. There is no standard procedure set aside by either OFAC or EU.

THE ALLOCATION OF COMPLIANCE RESPONSIBILITIES

This procedure identifies who in the organization is responsible for various aspects of sanctions compliance. In a sanctions compliance program, it is important to clearly define and allocate compliance responsibilities to ensure that the program is effectively implemented and enforced. Here are some common areas of responsibility in a typical compliance program:

- Senior management: Senior management is responsible for setting the tone at the top and ensuring that the organization's sanctions compliance policies and procedures are properly implemented, maintained, and reviewed. They are also responsible for allocating the necessary resources and support to the compliance function.

- Compliance officer: The compliance officer is responsible for the day-to-day oversight of the sanctions compliance program. They are responsible for ensuring that the program is properly designed, implemented, and operating effectively. They are also responsible for conducting risk assessments, developing policies and procedures, and providing training to staff.

- Operations and front-line staff: These staff members are responsible for carrying out the policies and procedures of the sanctions compliance program on a day-to-day basis. They are responsible for identifying and escalating potential sanctions risks and ensuring that all relevant policies and procedures are being followed.

- Legal: The legal department is responsible for providing legal advice on sanctions compliance matters. They are also responsible for reviewing and interpreting sanctions laws and regulations and ensuring that the organization's policies and procedures are consistent with them.

- Internal audit: The internal audit function is responsible for reviewing and testing the organization's sanctions compliance program to ensure that it is effective and operating as intended. They are also responsible for identifying any weaknesses or areas for improvement in the program.

- IT and data security: The IT department is responsible for ensuring that the organization's systems and data are secure and that the sanctions compliance program is properly integrated into these systems. They are also responsible for providing technical support to the compliance function.

- HR: The HR department is responsible for ensuring that all staff members are properly trained on the organization's sanctions compliance policies and procedures. They are also responsible for conducting background checks and due diligence on new staff members, particularly for positions that may be more susceptible to sanctions risk.

It is important to note that the allocation of compliance responsibilities may vary depending on the size and complexity of the organization, as well as the specific risks it faces. Ultimately, the goal is to ensure that all relevant staff members are aware of their responsibilities and are equipped to carry them out effectively.

MONITORING SANCTIONS RELATED DEVELOPMENTS

Monitoring changes to the applicable laws related to sanctions is an important part of sanctions compliance for businesses and organizations. The regulatory landscape is constantly changing, and sanctions lists and regulations are frequently updated, so it is important for organizations to stay up to date with the latest developments.

To monitor changes to sanctions laws and regulations, businesses can subscribe to alerts and updates from relevant regulatory bodies, such as OFAC, the EU, or the UN. They can also use third-party providers to help them monitor and stay up to date with sanctions changes.

In addition to monitoring sanctions lists and regulations, organizations should also conduct periodic risk assessments to identify changes in the sanctions landscape that may impact their business. This could include changes in the countries or individuals subject to sanctions, changes in the types of activities that are prohibited, or changes in the penalties for non-compliance.

By monitoring changes to the applicable laws related to sanctions, businesses can ensure that their compliance program remains up to date and effective, and that they are able to adapt quickly to any changes in the regulatory environment.

REVIEW OF EXISTING POLICIES

The review of existing policies is an essential component of an effective sanctions compliance program, as it helps to ensure that the organization remains compliant with applicable sanctions regulations and avoids costly penalties and reputational damage that can arise from non-compliance.

It is important that policies and procedures reflect the findings of risk assessments. This requires a procedure for reviewing existing policies and procedures after a risk assessment has been completed. Ideally, this will happen at least once a year.

CUSTOMER DUE DILIGENCE

Customer Due Diligence (CDD) is a critical component of any effective sanctions risk compliance program. CDD refers to the process of identifying and verifying the identity of customers and assessing their potential risks in relation to sanctions.

- Identification and Verification of Customers: A bank should have a process in place to identify and verify the identity of customers, including their name, address, and other relevant information. This may involve collecting documents such as passports, driving licenses, or other government-issued identification documents.

- Customer Risk Assessment: A bank should conduct a risk assessment of its customers to determine the level of risk they pose in relation to sanctions. The risk assessment should take into account factors such as the customer's country of origin, business activities, and potential exposure to sanctioned individuals or entities. To mitigate sanctions risks, it may be necessary to conduct some sort of due diligence regarding customers and potential customers, to ensure that they are not subject to sanctions.

BENEFICIAL OWNERSHIP CALCULATION

A beneficial owner is a person who can enjoy the same benefits as an owner of the company without actually being a legal owner. The most common example is being a shareholder or stakeholder of a company. These owners usually hold temporary ownership of part of a company and can influence their decisions and proceedings to an extent.

So, if any governmental or inter-governmental body sanctions a company, how will this affect the beneficial owners? According to the OFAC, these parties are only subject to sanctions if they own more than 50% stake in the sanctioned company.

50 Percent Rule, is a sanctions regulation that states that entities which are owned 50% or more by one or more

designated persons are also considered to be designated and subject to sanctions. The rule applies to both U.S. and non-U.S. entities, and it is intended to prevent designated individuals and entities from circumventing sanctions by using non-designated entities to conduct business.

Under the 50% Rule, if a designated person has a 50% or greater ownership interest in an entity, that entity is considered to be a "Blocked Person" and is subject to the same sanctions as the designated person. As a result, U.S. persons are generally prohibited from engaging in transactions with the blocked entity, unless licensed by OFAC. Non-U.S. persons may also be subject to secondary sanctions for engaging in certain transactions with blocked entities.

The 50% Rule is an important aspect of OFAC compliance, and entities must take steps to identify and screen their ownership structures and business partners to ensure compliance with the rule. This includes conducting due diligence on entities and individuals with whom they do business, and implementing sanctions screening procedures to identify and mitigate any potential risks. In many places, the legal owners are simply acting on behalf of the beneficial owners. The beneficial owners may not want their names to appear on public records. To ensure this, they do not assume legal ownership of an entity. In many cases, the beneficial owners may end up being criminals or sanctioned individuals. Hence, it is important to screen all owners- both on paper and off it.

Sanctioned entities and money-launderers usually deal in the same sectors. They mostly target areas where regulations are lax. This allows them to conduct illicit activities without undergoing extensive background checks and being caught. They commonly use shell companies, trade vehicles, or other inconspicuous methods to conduct their activities.

Many true owners also pose as beneficial owners to conceal their true identities. Hence, companies dealing with risky sectors must always conduct extensive due diligence so that they do not end up accidentally breaching sanctions. There are a variety of ways in which they can do so. The most common way to do so is to screen all clients against OFAC, OFSI, and UN watchlists.

REVIEW AND APPROVAL OF INDIVIDUAL TRANSACTIONS

Individual transactions in sanctions compliance refer to the screening of specific transactions to ensure that they do not violate any sanctions laws or regulations. This involves reviewing and verifying the details of the transaction, such as the names of the parties involved, the nature of the goods or services being traded, the country of origin and destination, and the method of payment.

Some of the examples of Individual transactions are:

- A company based in the US purchasing goods from a company based in Iran, which is a sanctioned country.
- A US-based bank transferring funds to an individual or entity that has been designated by OFAC as a Specially Designated National (SDN).
- A US-based company providing financial services to a company based in North Korea, which is a sanctioned country.
- A US-based individual providing consulting services to a company owned by a Russian oligarch who is subject to sanctions.
- A US-based company selling technology products to a company in Syria, which is a sanctioned country.

Depending upon the nature of an organization's business, it may be advisable to review at least some types of transactions that present a potential sanctions risk, and to require some sort of non-routine approval of medium- and high-risk transactions.

ASSIGNMENT OF RISK CLASSIFICATION

Classifying customers, business relations, and transactions as low, medium, or high risk allows an organization to devote its sanctions compliance resources to focusing on the riskiest.

Assigning risk classifications is an important part of a sanctions compliance program as it allows a financial institution to identify and prioritize higher risk clients, transactions, and activities. The risk classifications typically include low, medium, and high-risk categories, and are based on a range of factors, including the customer's location, industry, transaction history, and business relationships.

The risk classification process should be well-documented and transparent, and should be based on objective criteria that are consistent across the organization. Financial institutions should regularly review and update their risk classifications, especially as changes occur in the business, regulatory, or geopolitical landscape.

Once the risk classifications have been assigned, the financial institution can use this information to allocate compliance resources, such as enhanced due diligence, sanctions screening, and transaction monitoring, in proportion to the level of risk presented by each customer, transaction, or activity. This helps ensure that the most effective and efficient use of compliance resources is made to manage the institution's sanctions risks.

This requires a procedure explaining when and how the organization applies a risk classification.

APPLYING FOR A LICENSE

If the organization ever decided to do business with sanctioned countries, entities, or individuals, it may need a license to do so. This in turn requires a procedure that defines who makes the decision to apply for a license, and who is responsible for the application.

1. Maintaining information on what sanctions licenses and exemptions apply to the organization's business. Conversely, if licenses or exemptions apply to an organization's business, there must be readily available information within the organization regarding the scope of the license or exemption, as well as what procedures are required with respect to customers or transactions involving the license or exemption.

2. Handling transactions where a license authorizes an otherwise prohibited activity. Transactions subject to a license may require special measures, such as reporting to the authorities. This procedure should specify those measures.

3. Rejecting customers or transactions, including what the customer or counterparty should be told. Inherent in the review of customers and transactions is the possibility that customers will be declined or transactions rejected. A procedure should identify

who makes these decisions and what the customer or other parties are told about the decision. In general, it is considered wise to say as little as possible, so as not to give potential sanctions evaders any information about how an organization makes decisions regarding sanctions compliance.

RESOLVING DISPUTES WITHIN THE ORGANIZATION

Different parts of an organization may disagree over matters of sanctions compliance, such as whether a customer or transaction should be rejected. A procedure can specify how such disputes are resolved. To effectively resolve disputes within the organization, it is important to establish clear lines of communication and processes for escalation. This can include designating a specific point person or team to handle sanctions-related disputes and ensuring that all employees are aware of the process for raising concerns.

In addition, organizations should have a process for reviewing and resolving disputes, which may include seeking legal guidance or engaging with regulators or other relevant authorities. It is also important to document any disputes and the steps taken to resolve them, in order to demonstrate compliance efforts to regulators and other stakeholders.

ADMINISTERING FREEZING TRANSACTIONS

Persons in the EU, the United States, and other countries may be required by national law to freeze the funds or other assets of sanctioned parties.

Blocking or freezing transactions and administering frozen property is a crucial aspect of sanctions compliance for financial institutions. It involves the immediate suspension or blocking of transactions related to individuals, entities, or countries subject to sanctions, as well as the administration of any frozen property or assets.

Financial institutions must have effective procedures in place to identify, block, and report any transactions that involve individuals or entities on the sanctions list. They must also ensure that any frozen property or assets are administered in accordance with relevant laws and regulations.

The process of blocking transactions and administering frozen property typically involves the following steps:

- Identification: Financial institutions must have effective screening processes in place to identify transactions involving sanctioned individuals, entities, or countries. This may involve name screening, transaction monitoring, and other types of sanctions screening.
- Blocking: Once a transaction involving a sanctioned individual, entity, or country is identified, the financial

institution must immediately block the transaction. This involves preventing the transaction from being processed and notifying relevant authorities.

- Reporting: Financial institutions are required to report any blocked transactions to relevant authorities, such as the Office of Foreign Assets Control (OFAC) in the United States or the Financial Conduct Authority (FCA) in the United Kingdom. These reports must include detailed information about the transaction and the parties involved.

- Administering frozen property: Financial institutions must ensure that any frozen property or assets are administered in accordance with relevant laws and regulations. This may involve placing the assets in a special account or trust, limiting access to the assets, or transferring the assets to a designated authority. A procedure should identify when an asset must be frozen; exactly what the process is for freezing it (by placing in a special account, for example); and how the property is handled while it is frozen.

RECORDS RETENTION

Records retention rules are an important aspect of sanctions compliance. Financial institutions are required to maintain records related to their sanctions compliance program and transactions for a certain period of time. The length of time varies depending on the jurisdiction and the specific requirements of the regulatory agency.

In general, financial institutions should keep records related to sanctions compliance for at least five years. These records should include customer identification and due diligence information, transaction records, and any sanctions-related alerts, investigations, or resolutions.

It is important that these records are easily accessible and can be retrieved quickly in the event of an audit or investigation. Additionally, financial institutions should have processes in place to ensure that records are securely stored and protected from unauthorized access or tampering.

Failure to comply with records retention requirements can result in significant penalties and reputational damage. Therefore, it is important for financial institutions to establish and maintain robust records retention policies and procedures as part of their sanctions compliance program.

U.S. law, for example, requires that records regarding transactions potentially subject to sanctions be kept for five years. In addition, many organizations have their own records retention policies. The records retention procedure should identify

a. What records must be retained

b. How they will be retained (electronically, hard copy)

c. How long they must be retained

d. What should be done with them after the retention period has ended

TRAINING

Training plays a crucial role in sanctions compliance as it helps to ensure that all relevant employees within an organization understand the applicable sanctions regulations and their responsibilities in implementing and maintaining an effective sanctions compliance program.

Effective training should cover a range of topics, including the legal and regulatory framework for sanctions, the types of sanctions and their scope, sanctions screening and due diligence procedures, and the consequences of non-compliance with sanctions regulations.

Training should be provided to all employees whose job duties may involve sanctions-related activities, including front-line staff, compliance personnel, risk managers, and senior executives. It should also be provided on an ongoing basis to ensure that employees are aware of any changes to sanctions regulations or the organization's compliance policies and procedures.

PERIODIC REVIEW

The performance of periodic reviews of the operation of the sanctions compliance system requires its own detailed set of procedures. While Audit may be primarily responsible, the involvement of the compliance and legal functions is also necessary to ensure that the audit procedures reflect the legal requirements applying to the organization.

"WHISTLEBLOWER" PROCEDURES

There must be a procedure that enables personnel to report possible sanctions violations or practices against organization policy anonymously and without fear of retribution

The following are some key considerations when implementing whistleblower procedures in a sanctions compliance program:

- Confidentiality: Whistleblowers must have the option to report potential violations confidentially or anonymously. This is essential to encourage individuals to report violations without fear of retaliation.

- Non-Retaliation: Whistleblowers must be protected from retaliation, harassment, or discrimination in any form. It is important to have clear policies in place that outline the consequences of retaliating against whistleblowers.

- Accessibility: The reporting mechanism must be easily accessible to all stakeholders, including employees, clients, and other third parties.

- Investigation: Reported violations must be thoroughly investigated by an independent party to ensure that the issue is resolved and appropriate corrective action is taken.

- Escalation: If a potential violation is not resolved at the local level, there must be a mechanism in place to escalate the issue to senior management or the board of directors.

The procedure should specify when such an investigation should occur; who has the power to initiate it; who conducts the investigation; what the procedures for the investigation are; the form of the final report; who the report goes to; and who has the power to act upon the report.

CORRECTING WEAKNESSES IN SYSTEM

Correcting weaknesses demonstrates a good faith effort by the financial institution to comply with sanctions regulations. This can help to mitigate the impact of any potential violations and can help to build trust with regulators and other stakeholders.

Audits and internal investigations may identify deficiencies in the sanctions compliance system. A procedure should

194 | SANCTIONS SCREENING

ensure that, after the completion of an audit or an internal investigation, any deficiencies identified in the sanctions compliance system are corrected.

COMMUNICATIONS WITH CLIENTS.

Communication with clients on sanctions matters is a delicate issue. An organization may want customers to understand its overall policies, such as a refusal to do business with specific countries. However, it should not divulge too much information regarding either the overall operation of its sanctions compliance system or how it handles individual transactions, as such information can help sanctions evaders.

Client communication in the sanctions compliance is generally a five step process.

- Review the facts: Before reaching out to the client, make sure you have a clear understanding of the situation and the applicable sanctions regulations. Reach out to the client in a clear and professional manner to discuss the issue. Explain the sanctions requirements and how the client's actions are not in compliance.

- Provide guidance: Offer guidance on how the client can come into compliance with the sanctions regulations. This may involve providing information on specific transactions or actions that need to be avoided.

All Rights Reserved with Riskpro Publication

- Document the communication: It is important to document all communications with the client, including any guidance provided and the client's response.

- Follow up: Follow up with the client to ensure that they have taken steps to come into compliance with the sanctions regulations.

- Consider escalating: If the client continues to be non-compliant, it may be necessary to escalate the issue to senior management or to report the situation to the relevant regulatory authorities.

The communications procedure should detail what information will be provided to clients and business partners, especially with respect to individual transactions.

COORDINATION OF SANCTIONS POLICIES WITHIN A CORPORATE GROUP.

Members of a corporate group may well be located in different countries and subject to different sanctions regimes. It is important that a policy or procedure describe how they shall coordinate policies, and in particular whether and to what extent subsidiaries must comply with the sanctions laws of the corporate parent. OFAC has repeatedly penalized U.S. companies for violations of U.S. sanctions by their foreign affiliates

REPORTING

Reporting both regular and potential or actual violations is critical in sanctions compliance for several reasons:

- Compliance with regulations: Many regulations require companies to report any violations of sanctions laws or regulations. Failure to report violations can result in significant penalties and fines.

- Early detection of issues: Reporting potential or actual violations allows companies to identify issues early on, potentially mitigating the severity of the impact of the violation and enabling the company to take corrective action to prevent similar violations from occurring in the future.

- Demonstrating commitment to compliance: Reporting violations demonstrates a company's commitment to compliance with sanctions laws and regulations, which can be beneficial in building relationships with regulators, customers, and other stakeholders.

- Maintaining reputation: Timely reporting of violations can help to maintain the reputation of the company and prevent damage to its brand.

This may include such Key Performance Indicators as the number of transactions reviewed, the number rejected, the number of apparent violations observed, etc. In addition, a separate procedure should describe reports of potential violations.

REPORTING TO REGULATORS.

Depending upon the national law, organizations may be required to report to regulators instances where they have frozen assets or rejected transactions. A procedure should provide the details for this.

VOLUNTARY DISCLOSURES.

There may be times when an organization decides to voluntarily disclose to the appropriate authorities' potential sanctions violations.

It is worth noting, however, that voluntary disclosures should not be taken lightly and should only be made after a thorough internal investigation has been conducted. Companies should work closely with legal counsel to ensure that any disclosures are accurate, complete, and in compliance with applicable regulations.

The voluntary disclosure procedure should provide the details for this, including who has the authority to make a disclosure and what the disclosure should contain.

Practice Questions

What is the purpose of KYC requirements for the shipping industry?

A) To assess the risk of sanctions evasion.

B) To facilitate money laundering.

C) To evade regulatory compliance.

D) To increase the cost of doing business.

Answer: A

What is the OFAC 50% rule?

A) A rule that requires companies to identify and block transactions with entities owned 50% or more by individuals or entities on the OFAC sanctions list.

B) A rule that requires companies to provide 50% of their profits to OFAC.

C) A rule that requires companies to obtain permission from OFAC to do business with sanctioned individuals or entities.

D) A rule that requires companies to report any transactions with sanctioned individuals or entities to OFAC.

Answer: A

What is the e compliance program testing and auditing?

A) To avoid penalties for non-compliance.

B) To increase the risk of non-compliance.

C) To decrease the cost of compliance.

D) To identify gaps or deficiencies in the program.

Answer: A

What is the purpose of documenting testing and auditing activities in the sanctions compliance program?

A) To demonstrate compliance with regulatory requirements.

B) To facilitate non-compliance.

C) To decrease the cost of compliance.

D) To avoid penalties for non-compliance.

Answer: A

What is the KYV process?

A) The process of verifying the identity and ownership of a vessel and assessing its risk for sanctions evasion, smuggling, or other illicit activities.

B) The process of screening vessels for contraband.

C) The process of avoiding regulatory compliance.

D) The process of facilitating money laundering.

Answer: A

What is the purpose of screening vessels against sanctions lists in the KYV process?

A) To facilitate money laundering.

B) To identify vessels that are subject to sanctions.

C) To avoid regulatory compliance.

D) To increase the cost of doing business.

Answer: B

What is the purpose of conducting due diligence in the KYV process?

A) To increase the cost of doing business.

B) To facilitate non-compliance.

C) To assess the risk of non-compliance.

D) To avoid penalties for non-compliance.

Answer: C

What is the purpose of continuous improvement in the sanctions compliance program?

A) To update policies and procedures and enhance compliance.

B) To avoid penalties for non-compliance.

C) To facilitate non-compliance.

D) To decrease the cost of compliance.

Answer: A

AUTHOR PROFILES

Mayur Joshi

Mayur Joshi is a highly accomplished Chartered Accountant and graduate of commerce who has become a well-known figure in the field of forensic accounting in India. He has a wealth of qualifications, including a Certification in Forensic Accounting, Certification in Anti Money-laundering, Certification in Bank Forensic Accounting, and US certification in fraud examination.

Mayur is a strong advocate for forensic accounting in India and has won numerous awards for his work, including the international award in 2006 for Outstanding Achievement in Outreach/Community Service given by the Association of Certified Fraud Examiners. He was the first Indian professional to win an award from a professional association from United States.

In addition to his many accomplishments, Mayur has also served as a board member of ACFE India Chapter and the Vice President of ACFE- Western India chapter. He is a highly sought-after lecturer and has delivered talks on forensic accounting and fraud investigations in various prestigious institutions, including ISACA, ICAI, BMCC, Vaikunth Mehta College of Co-operative management, MIT school of management, SNDT Womens college of commerce, St. Meera's college, and many others.

Mayur is also a prolific writer and regularly contributes articles, knowledge-based resources, and experiences in the column on the success stories of the Certified Forensic Accounting Professionals. He has authored numerous books on the subject of frauds, which have been published by Indiaforensic Center of Studies and third-party publishers like Fraudexpress or Snow-white publishers.

Vedant Sangit

Vedant Sangit is Certified Anti Money Laundering Expert and a Regtech Evangelist. He is also an upcoming Script Writer and loves to write both professionally and as a hobby. Vedant Sangit is the co-founder of Regtech Times, a leading news portal on regulatory technologies. With a background in finance and accounting, Vedant noticed a gap in the market for information and news on the rapidly evolving field of regulatory technology. He co-founded Regtech Times in 2018 with the aim of providing comprehensive coverage of the latest developments in the field. Under his leadership, Regtech Times has become a go-to source of news and analysis for professionals in the regulatory technology industry, covering topics such as compliance, risk management, and cybersecurity. Vedant is also an entrepreneur and has launched several successful ventures in the past. He is passionate about technology and its ability to drive positive change in society.

REFERENCES

[i] https://regtechtimes.com/definitive-guide-to-sanctions/

[ii] https://www.justice.gov/opa/pr/former-abn-amro-bank-nv-agrees-forfeit-500-million-connection-conspiracy-defraud-united

[iii] https://www.justice.gov/opa/pr/ing-bank-nv-agrees-forfeit-619-million-illegal-transactions-cuban-and-iranian-entities

[iv] Extraterritoriality https://regtechtimes.com/courses/sanctions-violations/lessons/background-of-sanctions/topic/the-extraterritoriality-of-sanctions-and-blocking-statutes/

[v] https://finance.ec.europa.eu/eu-and-world/open-strategic-autonomy/extraterritoriality-blocking-statute_en#

[vi] EU Blocking Statute https://finance.ec.europa.eu/eu-and-world/open-strategic-autonomy/extraterritoriality-blocking-statute_en

[vii] https://www.coindesk.com/markets/2018/11/28/us-regulators-tie-two-bitcoin-addresses-to-iranian-ransomware-plot/

[viii] https://ofac.treasury.gov/recent-actions/20201230_33

[ix] https://www.swift.com/your-needs/financial-crime-cyber-security/why-sanctions-screening-so-important

[x] Wolfsberg Principles https://www.wolfsberg-principles.com/sites/default/files/wb/pdfs/Wolfsberg%20Guidance%20on%20Sanctions%20Screening.pdf

[xi] EU Sanctions List https://www.sanctionsmap.eu/#/main

[xii] UN Sanctions List https://www.un.org/securitycouncil/content/un-sc-consolidated-list

[xiii] UK OFSI Sanctions List https://www.gov.uk/government/publications/the-uk-sanctions-list

[xiv] DFAT Sanctions List https://www.dfat.gov.au/international-relations/security/sanctions/consolidated-list

[xv] CAATSA https://home.treasury.gov/policy-issues/financial-sanctions/sanctions-programs-and-country-information/countering-americas-adversaries-through-sanctions-act-related-sanctions

[xvi] HKMA Sanctions https://www.hkma.gov.hk/eng/key-functions/banking/anti-money-laundering-and-counter-financing-of-terrorism/sanctions-related-notices-updates/

[xvii] Know Your Vessel https://regtechtimes.com/know-your-vessel/

[xviii] Equasis Database https://www.equasis.org/EquasisWeb/public/About?fs=HomePage&P_ABOUT=Providers.html

Made in United States
Orlando, FL
26 October 2023

38236072R00114